Ethnicity, Citizenship & State in Eastern Africa

Aquiline Tarimo, S.J.

Langaa Research & Publishing CIG
Mankon, Bamenda

Publisher:
Langaa RPCIG
Langaa Research & Publishing Common Initiative Group
P.O. Box 902 Mankon
Bamenda
North West Region
Cameroon
Langaagrp@gmail.com
www.langaa-rpcig.net

Distributed outside N. America by African Books Collective
orders@africanbookscollective.com
www.africanbookcollective.com

Distributed in N. America by Michigan State University Press
msupress@msu.edu
www.msupress.msu.edu

ISBN: 9956-579-99-8

CONTENTS

PREFACE

The African civil wars have killed millions of people, destroyed property, and strained social relationships between ethnic communities. Many initiatives were launched to contain the situation, and some of them created lasting impact. Meanwhile, the number of militia groups and refugees appear to be decreasing gradually. In the near future, perhaps, political stability could be achieved. Such a situation suggests that there would be no need of peacekeeping missions and non-governmental organizations created to address the plight of refugees and internally-displaced people. The emerging challenge is how to promote political integration and equal citizenship in a condition where millions of people are unsettled and disorganized.

It would, however, take time to achieve such an objective because of the existing mistrust between ethnic groups and unjust social structures. The situation suggests that the process of peacemaking has already entered another stage, a stage of character formation. If this is the case, then the challenge of character formation and institutionalization of democracy, through citizenship education, has automatically become the task of all institutions. Such engagement will require those institutions that form public conscience, through the cultivation of religious virtues and civic virtues, to play a formative role. Reform of cultural traditions is required because some methodologies of political organization tend to advocate destructive competition and mutual hostility that undermine the effort of promoting responsible citizenship.

There has been a growing need to evaluate the impact of ethnicity on citizenship due to the problems related to state legitimacy and governance. These problems are common among multicultural societies that find it difficult to organize themselves as nation-states. The dynamics of ethnicity and citizenship are also implicated in the phenomena of forced migration, urbanization, statelessness, and exclusion. The situation has been caused by armed conflicts that dominated the political life of many counties in the last three decades. I am raising these issues to alert the policymakers on the need of acknowledging the demands of citizenship rights as a means of promoting participatory democracy. The discussion unveils paradigms of civic engagement that can promote a new understanding of ethnicity and citizenship, formation of public conscience, and rebuilding of social relationships. From such a perspective I argue that promotion of responsible citizenship is indispensable for political advancement.

To address the challenges of forced migration, exclusion, and conflict I propose to evaluate the impact of ethnicity on citizenship because these variables determine the meaning of citizenship rights. Its role within the public sphere remains ambiguous and problematic. With such a background I argue that the functions performed through the dynamics of ethnic identification toward political integration cannot be overlooked. It is from such a perspective that the study examines the impact of the politics of ethnicity and citizenship on the process of political integration.

This study, while rooted in interdisciplinary scholarship, is not a study in normative political theory; rather, as a study in applied political ethics, its objective is to identify relevant moral norms that could be used to promote political transformation. To gain a perspective about the nature and influence of the politics of ethnicity, the analysis draws concrete examples from Eastern Africa countries as an empirical case to show the extent to which ethnicity influences the politics of citizenship. The analysis, while focusing on the post-conflict period, could enlighten those struggling to resolve complex challenges related to immigration and citizenship rights.

The completion of this volume is made possible through the collaboration of many people. Through such collaboration it has become possible to complete this volume, which I believe will be valuable for scholars and students engaged in peace studies, international relations, migration and citizenship studies, political philosophy, and political theology. The volume unveils an academic approach that constitutes an important ingredient in the constant drive to transform the politics of ethnicity and citizenship. In a special way, my hearty thanks are due to Dr. Margaret G. Gecaga, currently lecturing at Kenyatta University, Nairobi, Kenya. She provided me with valuable critiques, corrections, and suggestions. I am also indebted to Dr. Paulin Manwelo, S.J., the former Director of the Institute of Peace Studies and International Relations at Hekima College, Nairobi, for his academic insights that motivated the idea of writing this volume. I am also indebted to Dr. Felix M. Kiruthu, Lecturer in the Department of History, Kenyatta University, for the correction of the manuscript and critique. Finally, I cannot forget Dr. Laurenti Magesa for his invaluable suggestions.

1. Introduction: Institutionalization of Ethnicity

In Africa, while rich in human and natural resources, many people are still left to wallow in hunger, disease, and conflict. These problems are mainly the product of human activities and decisions undertaken by people who have no regard for the common good. Such a situation occurs through a tragic complicity and criminal conspiracy between local leaders and foreign agents. The origin of such a shameful involvement derives from the fact that some political leaders pursue wealth and privilege at the expense of the people they lead. Whatever may be the responsibility of foreign agents there is always a shameful involvement of local leaders who sell out their countries to unscrupulous foreign agents.

The appropriate response to the prevailing condition of political instability requires concerted effort geared to make people agents of social change. There is a need to promote effective modalities of leadership and governance sustained by spirituality and political dynamics founded upon multidimensional and interdisciplinary programs of civic education and formation of public conscience. Initiatives of change require evaluation and innovation. With expectation, this book attempts to engage the prevailing political conditions to spark dialogue that could lead toward improved awareness, commitment, and action. A creative response seeks to define reality, not to suspend it, while encouraging innovation as a means to overcome uncertainty and vulnerability.

Disputes characterized by unequal distribution of wealth, competing identities, and the lack of participation in decision-making process cannot be fully resolved by relief programs and readymade methodologies borrowed from abroad. Similarly, the task of promoting a cohesive political society cannot depend entirely on the voluntary initiative emerging from externally-oriented organizations. A search for a long-term solution to the disintegration of political institutions entails a collective initiative geared toward transformation of value systems and establishment of cohesive socio-political institutions. The struggle for political transformation requires a collective determination founded upon public reason. In order to achieve such an objective, a proper union of these variables ought to take into account the diversity of ethnic identities. The following introduction outlines the nature of the problem and context, methodology and scope, objective and presentation, and significance and relevance of the study to the African context.

Problem and Context

The term "ethnicity" is difficult to define because it is composed of overlapping attributes instead of a single cultural trait. Ethnic community refers to a group of people sharing a common ancestry, language, belief, myth, custom, history, kinship, territory, and other distinctive attributes. These variables serve as a ground for identity, loyalty, security, and hostility to others. Ethnic identity derives its foundation from combined memories of the past, blood ties, and common expectation. Many people continue to lead their lives within the framework of an ethnic group. When a person is in difficulties, it is normal for this person to call for help from the ethnic community to which he belongs. In urban areas ethnic identity is appealed to when people are in need of financial and political support. For many people ethnic identity stands as a symbol of solidarity and security. Ethnic identity, be it in rural or urban areas, remains a powerful force to reckon with, although it varies like temperature, from time to time, depending on prevailing political circumstances. It is a fluid concept, meaning different things at different times and contexts.

Characteristics of ethnicity include mutual suspicion, vicious cycle of deep-rooted hatred, and exclusion. All these forms of social relationships are deeply influenced by the fight for social status, inadequate resources, and competing identities. Political instability obstructs economic advancement, social integration, and political stability. They reveal tensions arising from the experience of injustice related to unequal distribution of resources and disputes about status. They, however, occur in search for a transformative change. Some of them are deliberately created to sustain practices of exploitation and corruption. In search for a long-term solution, each situation needs to be studied in terms of its own dynamics, context, and interest at stake for the parties involved. There is no simple prescription in addressing the challenge of political integration because one is dealing with the complexity of social relationships.

The politicization of ethnicity and citizenship continues to foment tendencies of exclusion and marginalization over issues of wealth distribution and power sharing. The situation is basically shaped by the competition between cultural and religious identities. In order to overcome the situation, coupled with concerted effort to rebuilt crippled institutions, the entire population must be involved. Together with localized initiatives, people must be assisted to implement localized strategy geared toward a reform founded upon institutionalization of broad-based modalities of participation. In the process of addressing the multilayered politicization of ethnicity and citizenship, variables of mutual accommodation and inclusion are crucial for any effort intending to promote political cohesion, peace, and justice.

The causes of political disintegration originate not only from outside but also from inside because of the disordered loyalties and interests between ethnic groups. From the viewpoint of social organization, such a situation could be linked to the fragmentation of the value systems, inability to establish social order, and the lack of an agreed-upon concept of the common good. The situation renders administrative systems incapable of addressing fundamental needs of political life such as freedom of expression, participation in decision-making process, and power sharing. The effects that emerge from the situation include corruption, breakdown of the state authority, and irresponsible leadership. The dynamics of political instability propagate reciprocal causation through which the response mechanism becomes the means to perpetuate the cycle of violence, especially where people have experienced mutual hostility for a long time. Where there is a long-term experience of mistrust people are susceptible to manipulation.

The lack of political cohesion appears to be characterized by conditions of competing identities, loyalties, and interests. The conflict of interests exacerbates the situation when added to economic hardships. Such disputes are difficult to resolve through negotiation and compromise. They may be interrupted by political agreements, but such initiatives could break down very easily by falling into low-intensity warfare accompanied with endless hostilities. The increase of mutual hostility complicates the process of political integration by creating an atmosphere bereft of constructive engagement. The political manipulation, in many ways, exacerbates the situation by appealing to ethnic identities as a way of building political ambitions. As the rivalry between ethnic groups builds, each side dramatizes and magnifies the mistrust between them and eventually transforms the tension into a conflict. The growing mistrust and pain they have inflicted on each other make it difficult for parties involved to sit down and engage in a dialogue that can establish a reasonable agreement. The situation keeps growing, and new challenges keep emerging that could prevent the achievement of any meaningful agreement.

In view of addressing the situation of political instability, the Organization of African Unity took an initiative of appointing leaders to facilitate the process of dialogue and settling political dispute within the society. Since the 1980s, when the initiative was launched, there has been insignificant achievement. Despite the failure, it is appropriate to draw a lesson from this initiative by proposing approaches that can address the situation effectively. Such an engagement requires adequate knowledge upon which transformative models of political organization could be based.

Methodology and Scope

Critics claim that ethical methodology stifle human spirit, obstruct creativity, and prevent people from raising new questions. While accepting such a reminder, we must also bear in mind that each methodology is limited because it cannot accommodate all perspectives and interests, and that scattered ideas require a methodological synthesis. Methodologies help us to synthesize a variety of sources and ideas by shaping various modes of reflection that motivate social action. Such an engagement directs various approaches towards a prism of synthesis as a way of uniting different dimensions of human experience. Methodological analyses are necessary in understanding strategies adopted to promote social transformation. Methodology is an important tool of research because it provides a guideline for reasoning, systematization, and evaluation. It provides the capacity to comprehend the patterns of value systems as well as identify structures that need innovation. Without a methodological guidance, scholars and practitioners alike could be lost in scattered descriptions, thereby failing to identify methodologies that can change the situation.

Regarding methodologies of addressing political disintegration, confusion, and conflict, a number of the existing methodologies seem to be incapable to address crucial issues such as the source of ethnic hatred and the urge for revenge. Methodologies that have been applied could be categorized as temporary initiatives intended to resettle the population rather than solve the problem completely. In the end, the root causes of the confusion, hatred, and conflict remain unresolved. There is a necessary interplay between governance and democratization. We cannot fully address one of these subjects without considering the import of the other. Such theories fail to examine the role of traditions and institutions designed to promote a democratic culture. The dynamics of political transformation are expected to assume the task of restructuring social relationships, value systems, and attitudes to facilitate reconstruction of collective identity. The widespread initiatives that have been undertaken tend to concentrate on collecting empirical data focused on political events. Likewise, a number of the prevailing political discourses do not address the root causes of the situation. Methodologies that have been applied tend to ignore the need to establish multidimensional and interdisciplinary approaches derived from indigenous cultures as a means to construct a localized foundation. Such flaws emerge from the fact there are no critical evaluations designed to demonstrate strengths and limitations resulting from the prevailing approaches. The studies being undertaken to explore the political situation seem to lack analyses that can demonstrate a shift from confusion, misunderstanding, and conflict to the task of building a democratic culture.

The issue of methodology cannot be taken for granted in social sciences because it determines the input of scientific principles guiding the intellectual enterprise and application. A number of studies tend to focus on a single methodology while forgetting that there are other valuable methodologies ranging from diplomacy to spirituality. Different societies require different methodologies because each crisis has its own set of causes, and as such a single approach cannot be relevant to all contexts. In addition to that political initiatives seem to be sporadic and removed from the people concerned. It is worthy noting that there are different methodologies of resolving political instability within the context of competing identities, loyalties, and interests. A localized approach based upon rational dialogue across socio-political institutions can reduce uncertainty in the way of proceeding. Such a consideration is crucial because a number of written accounts seem to be scattered and artificial. A number of scholars are confined within a single institution, field of study, and perspective with a possibility of forgetting that a human person is subjected to an array of interrelated experiences arising from different institutions. With the aim to formulate a comprehensive literature, an integral approach could enrich the ongoing discourse on political reform.

The horizon of the methodological evaluation employed in the investigation, in search for a long-term solution to the political instability, calls upon political theories to promote a culture that is open to change, both in systems of thought and attitude. Concerning the process of pursuing such an objective I wish to argue that transformation of the models of social organization plays a significant role in the effort of promoting political transformation. The project ought to draw social actors toward the challenge of linking value systems with political strategies designed to overcome the politics of disorder. It introduces those concerned into the search for a long-term solution by unveiling the root causes of the situation. The horizon of the examination develops an account that is multidimensional by the virtue of using sources drawn from different fields of study. Such an argument allows us to bring together sources from cultural anthropology, political philosophy, international relations, and public theology. The process of addressing political instability is not only a matter of healing memories, organizing elections, writing constitutions, or forming coalition governments; rather, it is about shifting the political landscape, restructuring institutions, and molding public conscience.

The approach employed in the book could be categorized as evaluative, multidimensional, cross-cultural, and interdisciplinary. An approach of this kind could be effective because it allows different experiences to converge in search for appropriate and lasting solutions. The horizon accommodates different dimensions of human experience and diversity of social relationships with the aim of transcending the polarity between different kinds of justice. It also focuses on character formation instead of being limited to the external dimension of social relationships and political events.

The option to merge sources drawn from various fields of study is worthy of note, because it incorporates in itself a number of variables emerging from different dimensions of human experience. Such a process moves from the level of description to the level of analysis, interpretation, and appropriation as a means to converge theory and practice. The study does not only reveal the root causes of the problem, but also proposes a viable solution. An approach of this sort is required because a number of the prevailing methodologies within the domain of social sciences tend to concentrate on describing socio-political events. This is because the life of a human person is always subjected to a multitude of experiences arising from different institutions. Without recourse to virtues we cannot reform public morality. Engagement of this kind could be interpreted as a process of consolidating different models of participation, identifying the root causes, and planning for appropriate action.

The scope of the investigation seeks to stimulate public opinion about possibilities that could promote creative thinking as well as empower policymakers to formulate development policies that can effectively address the vicious cycle of hatred-violence-revenge. The process of innovation requires transformation of value systems and institutions as a means to create a long-term solution. Such an objective could be achieved insofar as the majority of people engage themselves in activities that encourage grassroots participation. Such a demand confirms the claim that we must put blame on our own shortcomings instead of shifting the full responsibility to foreign agents. The process of political transformation is an enterprise that requires those concerned to establish conditions that can enable them to take charge of their life by focusing on long-term solutions. Without taking such an orientation, short-term initiatives can only temporarily relieve the situation; they cannot bring forth a significant long-term change.

The methodology employed in this volume navigates between development theories and socio-cultural critical theory with the purpose of motivating an involvement that can create innovative political culture. It correlates thinking models, cultural traditions, and belief systems with prevailing political conditions. With the aim to pave a way for the future, the discourse puts an accent on the need to promote ethics of innovation. The envisioned horizon of social action allows the discussion to progress further with the aim of enlightening people on the importance of developing localized methodologies of participation and self-governance. True formation helps a person to discover realities of life as well as develop skills of survival. Such a model of formation helps the mind to grow in search for truth, self-discovery, and self-actualization. It promotes moral maturity in the way we address political challenges. The horizon of this kind supports the claim that Africa must challenge itself if it is to avoid self-destruction and impoverishment.

Objective and Presentation

The objective of the study, from Eastern Africa perspective, which includes Tanzania, Kenya, Uganda, Rwanda, Burundi, Sudan, Ethiopia, Eritrea, and Somalia, is to examine the impact of the politics of ethnicity on the processes of political integration and citizenship. In order to concretize the investigation the analysis of the relationship between ethnicity, citizenship, and nationalism becomes imperative. The scope of the project engages relational aspects of social life, awakens public conscience, and motivates civic engagement. Such a tentative inquiry could be useful not only for resolving ongoing disputes, but also for rebuilding social relationships. This is, in fact, a post-conflict project designed to envision the future of the African states. The test of its validity and usefulness is not whether it accounts for particular conflicts, but whether it provides a framework through which we can comprehend the dynamics of political integration.

This volume is organized into six chapters. The first chapter, which forms the introductory part of the book, examines the dynamics attached to the process of institutionalizing ethnicity. Such an engagement presents a framework that defines the problem and context, methodology and scope, objective and presentation, and the relevance of the study to the African situation today.

The second chapter focuses on politicization of ethnic identities by taking into account historical, cultural, economic, and political variables that form the background of the situation. The discussion opens the stage by unveiling the problem and context through which the discourse is situated. It begins by arguing that one of the challenges tearing Africa countries apart includes the tendency to manipulate ethnic identities for private interest. We can grasp the root causes of the prevailing ethno-political competition, discrimination, and conflict insofar as we take seriously the following questions. How is ethnic identity related to the conflict of loyalties and interests? How have the dynamics of ethnic identities fashioned the existing understanding of the common good and political life? Have religions, including Christian churches, managed to stand above ethnocentrism and the tension it generates? In search for long-term solutions to these questions, this investigation demonstrates how ill-founded methodologies tend to sideline equal citizenship among citizens in favor of the model of exclusion founded upon ethnic affiliation. The challenge of integrating cultural identities in the process of political integration is closely related to the problematic concepts of ethnicity, citizenship, nation-state, and common good.

The third chapter accounts for the conditions underlying the connection between ethnic diversity and political integration, under which ethno-political competition revolves, which bears three common denominators, namely, identity, loyalty, and interest. The argument unveiled in the discussion, as a response to the challenge of political integration, is that contemporary Africa needs politics that depend more upon public reason, dialogue, and consensus than blood relationship. The study opens the inquiry by examining the dynamics of ethnic politics followed by relationship between corruption and ethnicity. Such an analysis intends to show that ethnocentrism is partially perpetuated by economic factors through the practice of corruption. The second part of the discussion attempts to justify the claim that democracy is an attitude of mind, and as such a serious promotion of democracy must concentrate on transforming the mind which effect social relationships. The third part evaluates a number of proposed possibilities intending to apply the principle of federalism to overcome ethnocentrism and rivalry. The last two parts put an emphasis on the need of respecting cultural diversity as a means to enhance political integration and democratic accountability.

The fourth chapter, with the aim of rescuing the future from the current situation, concentrates on promoting transformative education for responsible citizenship, mutual accommodation, and community service by evaluating the impact of the prevailing tension between ethnic politics, citizenship, and self-determination. The objective of such an engagement is to justify the claim that the formation of citizens is the foundation of political integration, because social actions reveal the commitment of the citizens toward one another. Transformation of political life requires a formation that can inculcate among the citizens the sense of mutual respect and the common good.

The fifth chapter examines the relationship between religion, politics, and civil society. Although the effort of appealing to religion to promote inter-institutional collaboration and political integration is constructive, we must also acknowledge that the role of religion in the public sphere is limited. The relationship between the attitude of exclusion, religion, and civil society, from the perspective of promoting political integration, is problematic because a number of people regard religion as a conversation-stopper, irrational, divisive, and uncivil. Critics claim that religions are too rigid and authoritative in addressing social issues, to the extent that it is almost impossible to engage them in a meaningful dialogue. On the other side of the divide, the opinion is that religions have always played significant roles in the political process. The two opposing positions have left the relationship between religion and civil society undefined, even when collaborative action is required to save life. The discussion, from the context of Eastern Africa countries, attempts to unveil the root causes of the situation as well as propose methodologies that can address the situation effectively.

The sixth chapter unveils fundamental values upon which public values are founded. Such a perspective is brought into the discussion to play the role of unveiling ethical principles required for guidance in the process of establishing a framework upon which political integration is founded. It extends further the search for appropriate methodologies by focusing on the character formation as an important aspect for addressing political instability. Such a perspective aims at helping the reader to recognize that methodologies that can effectively address the root cause of political instability must be situated at the level of value system. With a presupposition that rights-claims are founded upon fundamental values, the framework of the analysis justifies the claim that the process of political integration is a constitutive dimension of democracy that transcends ethnic politics.

Significance and Relevance of the Study

The study brings forth insights that could be used to promote education for citizenship, political cohesion, and moral formation. It unveils difficulties encountered by the movements of nationalism with the aim of proposing models of governance that could be useful in the process of political integration. The horizon of this investigation takes seriously transformation of attitudes of the people involved toward one another as a reliable paradigm of building a cohesive political society. In so doing the investigation could enhance fulfillment of the desires of the people, especially the longing for political leaders who would be public servants able to practice the art of bringing diverse ethnic communities together. In a situation where bonds of grassroots communities are fractured, the most basic virtues of tolerance, responsibility, and integrity seem to be collapsing, thereby losing values underlying the ethics of the common good. With such a situation at hand we have to do everything possible to promote values that can challenge the prevailing enmity between social groups. Such an orientation can

11

help us to construct a political framework founded upon ethical principles of the common good and collective responsibility.

The exploration proposes three dimensions of understanding the challenges surrounding the process of political integration, namely, ethnicity, citizenship, and religion. These dimensions are closely interrelated and constitute characteristics that contribute to the prevailing political situation. The prevailing political crises raise challenges that necessitate critical reflection. In so doing we may be able to answer the following questions. First, given the generalized poverty, ignorance, and ethnic rivalry, most often the ability to lead is not determined by merit, but by ethnic affiliation; and if that is the case, then, what forms of democracy and governance are appropriate for Africa? Second, with the prevalent logic of the politics of the belly that compromises ethics of the common good, how do we translate fundamental values into social structures? For Africa, the effort of molding unified political entities beyond ethnic borders remains elusive. Neither a simple coalition government, nor a power-sharing formula based upon ethnic affiliation will be able to overcome the lack of socio-political cohesion. In the life of each nation, structural reforms must be carried out as a means of responding to the changing conditions of life. If public authorities are reluctant to carry out serious reforms, then the ongoing political strife will prevail. What distinguishes democratic governance from autocratic governance is the ability to undertake a reform geared to enhance communication between people in a peaceful manner.

Insights resulting from the inquiry could be used as a resource for the formation of the public conscience. Such a perspective concentrates on promoting institutions that can formulate contextual methodologies of educating the population about the art of organizing complex societies. A framework of this kind promotes education for responsible citizenship and formation of social actors who can manage diversity in a way that can enhance mutual accommodation. To this end, the study brings forth a framework that can inform practice by identifying effective methodologies of political integration.

2. Politicization of Ethnic Identities

The problems challenging contemporary Africa are numerous, and some of them are cultural in the sense that they are related to cherished practices inherited from indigenous cultures. It could be argued that such problems do not only result from the imposition of the European colonial rule with its concomitant introduction of European cultural values and institutions; rather, some of the problems are related to the African capacity to grapple with the changing conditions of life, especially the challenge to integrate ethnic identities into the structure of nation-state.

The tendency of manipulating ethnic identities for private interest can thoroughly be understood insofar as we take seriously the following questions. How is ethnic identity related to the conflict of loyalties and interests? How have the dynamics of ethnic identities shaped the existing understanding of the common good and political integration? Have religions, including Christianity, managed to stand above ethnocentrism and the tension it generates? Given the importance of these questions the root cause of ethno-political competition, discrimination, and conflict deserves a critical examination. The focus and structure of this chapter follow the framework of the aforementioned questions.

Ethno-Political Competition, Discrimination, and Conflict

Kenya, for example, is a multi-ethnic society, and many communities have lived in harmony for many years. In recent years, however, the dominant ethnic groups have been on the forefront in fighting for political power.[1] The situation has resulted into fighting to control the state. The relatively less dominant communities have been playing the card of opportunism. Historically, many ethnic groups supported the armed struggle for independence in hope that they could regain their stolen lands. This expectation did not become reality. The situation fomented anger, resentment, lust for revenge, and aggressive competitiveness that overlooked the common good of the entire country. Frustration among the poor, both in urban and rural areas, created a growing tendency to use violence as a viable means to change the situation. When violent reactions emerge, under the influence of ethno-political ideologies, they tend to take the form of ethnocentrism, the ideology that animates the competition between ethnic groups.

A section of the population was unhappy about the outcome of the election of December, 2007, but, to a certain extent, the occasion presented a chance to correct some of the historical wrongs committed against certain communities.[2] Injustice occurred in the area of land ownership and distribution, when land was confiscated from the indigenous people by British settlers and later retaken by politically powerful personalities after independence in 1963. Instead of returning the stolen lands to the original owners, the politically connected personalities benefited the occasion of the departing white settlers to grab land, while relegating those who owned the land before the white settlers came to the category of the landless. Reactions of discontent were revealed in the land clashes of 1992, 1997, and 2007.[3] These clashes displayed the anger among those living in impoverished conditions. Others were also frustrated because of the deliberate delay in addressing structural injustices haunting the society since independence.

Ethno-political competition, which has been alive for a long time, has finally degenerated into ethno-political violence, discrimination, and conflict.[4] Ever since the flawed election triggered a wave of ethno-political violence many people have been violently driven from their homes and many are now resettling in ethnically homogenous zones. Even some of the packed slums in certain cities are split along ethnic lines.[5] Ethnic demarcation and regionalism, as promoted by ethnic leaders, revolve around the practice of ethnic discrimination. The phenomenon of ethnic discrimination comes into play when each region is identified with a certain ethnic group, and whenever political misunderstandings emerge those who are identified as foreigners are always forced to go to their ancestral land. Macharia Gaitho presents the impact of ethno-political competition, discrimination, and violence saying: "We are our own perverse version of regionalism by forcing certain ethnic groups to leave certain regions exclusive to the supposedly indigenous communities."[6] We are witnessing, on a massive scale, the forced movement of people back to their supposedly ancestral homelands. This phenomenon raises serious question of whether some countries will ever continue to exist as a modern nation-state, or whether they will be going back to the pre-colonial stage of ethnic fiefdoms with no central authority. That is the consequence of the politics based on ethnic identities instead of moral principles that hold modern democracies together. Instead of evolving, politically speaking, most of the African democracies have regressed to produce ethnic leaders focused on leading their people in warfare against rival communities. The political crisis, under the influence of ethnic rivalry and revenge, killed many people and destroyed property, including burning of houses. Such a crisis erupted due to the lack of peaceful means to address grievances. The condition was aggravated by the lack of the rule of law, socio-political cohesion, and responsible leadership.

Ethno-political violence is a deliberate political strategy created by desperate groups intended to effect change in the political system that marginalizes them. The situation has emerged because of unequal distribution of resources, unabated corruption at the national level, extreme poverty in urban slums and squatters, unemployment, and irresponsible leadership. The situation is combined with the political unwillingness to address structural injustice. The inability to go beyond the ethnic framework has intensified the climate of political crisis.[7] For John Githongo, the former Director of the Kenya Anti-Corruption Commission, "the country's leadership is responsible, not just the political leadership but also the cultural and religious leaders. Among them, there are those that have allowed their love of power to overwhelm the common good."[8] The phenomenon of ethno-political competition, discrimination, and conflict is not limited to Kenya. It has also been experienced in Rwanda, Burundi, Somalia, Ethiopia, and elsewhere within the continent of Africa. In order to address the problem we have to device effective methodologies that can promote inclusive structures of the common good, wealth distribution, and political participation. There will be no lasting peace unless each country "addresses the fundamental inequalities that turn neighbor against neighbor and ethnic group against ethnic group."[9] The following analysis attempts to outline the main characteristics that fashion politicization of ethnic identities and the root causes of ethno-political competition, discrimination, and conflict in contemporary Africa.

Competing Identities, Loyalties, and Interests

The meaning of ethnic identity is difficult to grasp unless we relate it to the changing conditions of life.[10] One has to consider the cultural, socio-economic, and political changes that have been taking place and how they have continued to fashion ethnic identities, loyalties, and interests. Ethnic identities, from the African perspective, assume a triple history: pre-colonial, colonial, and post-colonial. In the pre-colonial period, ethnic groups were rural and homogeneous, and there was less competition between them for the scarce economic resources than it is today. In the pre-colonial period, remarks John Lonsdale, there was a recognized art of living in a reasonably peaceful way without a state structure in the way it is understood today.[11] In some countries, small ethnic groups, during the colonial period, were forced to merge.

Loyalty is naturally connected to the sense of commitment that could be categorized as a devotion of a person to a cause sustained practically. Loyalty involves willingness, commitment, and service. It is a submission of one's desire to a particular cause that provides guidance. If one is loyal, then he has a cause which he personally values. Loyalty is attached to a bond of relationship that is internal, and tends to unify life and give it identity and stability. You cannot be loyal to a merely impersonal abstraction; and you also cannot be loyal simply to a collection of divided persons, viewed merely as a collection.[12] Where there is an object of loyalty there is a union of selves into one life. Such a union constitutes a cause to which one may indeed be loyal. Loyalty is always connected to interests expressed in terms of identity, solidarity, and security.

Identity refers to loyalty for a particular culture, religion, community, or tradition. It is a medium through which people define themselves vis-à-vis other groups as well as reinforce patterns of social relationships between members of a given community. Through collective identity, however, one group may consider itself better than the other, thereby creating boundaries between social groups. Identity can be used to divide people into competing groups. The process of changing the identity sphere of relationship may mean redefining the boundaries that distinguish people. Changing identity appeals to the evaluation of differences, attitudes, and relationships between social groups. It could be seen as a process of political process that shapes social perception, interaction, and organization. Changing identity involves flexibility in the way one understands and relates to others in the society. It is about re-ordering patterns of social interaction and commitment to the common good and changing social relationships.

Concepts of identity and loyalty, as markers of one's worldview, have significant implications for the formation of cohesive political society. The prevailing experiences of the disintegration of political institutions and conflicts confirm that there is a need to challenge traditions that render the concept of ethnicity problematic. It is evident that identities are socially constructed, reinforced, renegotiated, and deconstructed. Such a confirmation supports the claim that it is appropriate to deconstruct certain traditions upon which ethnic identity is built. Such a project must engage everyone in the process of redefining ethnic identity in a way that is liberating. It is an initiative that requires all to break the interlocking systems of outdated traditions inherited from the past. We cannot live in harmony without propagating a political culture characterized by rational dialogue, public reason, and mutual accommodation. Transformative paradigms of this sort require everyone to challenge inherited structures of political organization.

Because of the ethnic competition for the scarce economic resources and political power, each ethnic group tends to fight to have a president from their group.[13] For them, the president will manipulate state machinery to benefit his ethnic group. In other words, the president is not for the state, but his ethnic group. This is the root cause of the struggle to control the state. Ethnic strategies are often connected with the resources of modern economy, such as in gaining employment, education, securing loans, and seizing appointments for lucrative offices. The competition for the limited economic resources within the state today, to a certain extent, has changed the meaning of ethnic identities.

Ethnicity is one of the most difficult concepts to grasp, and one of the most essential in understanding contemporary Africa. David Lamb argues that African leaders deplore ethnocentrism in public by calling it the cancer that threatens to eat out the very fabric of the nation.[14] Yet almost every African politician practices it. Experience shows that most African presidents are more ethnic chief than national statesman, and it remains perhaps the most potent force in day-to-day African life. It is a factor in political struggles and distribution of resources. It often determines who gets jobs, who gets promoted, who gets accepted to a university, because by its very definition ethnicity implies sharing among members of the extended family, making sure that your own are looked after first. To give a job to a fellow ethnic member is not nepotism, it is an obligation.[15] For a political leader to choose his closest advisers and bodyguards from the ranks of his own ethnic group is not patronage, it is a good common sense. It guarantees security, loyalty, and control. The challenge is not how to overcome ethnic identities, but how to integrate them into social relationships and political organization. The effort of promoting democracy cannot succeed without taking into account the challenge of appropriating ethnic identities into the structure of nation-state. Any project, be it political, economic, or religious, which involves the mobilization of people must take into account the cultural contexts in which individuals live, rather than those in which someone may think they ought to be living. We can remove people from a village, not a village from them. The process of building democratic institutions will succeed insofar as it starts with what people are and from where they come from.

Many studies of ethnicity tend to concentrate on justifying the claim that any political organization based on ethnic identity is a primitive model. In most cases such approaches suggest that if Africa wants to make progress it must first of all eradicate ethnicity. Consequently a number of the African political leadership put an accent on assimilation, rather than inclusion and acceptance of difference as the only approach to national unity.[16] Because of such influence, many leaders think that ethnic identities will disappear as the process of urbanization gains momentum. They conceive the existence of ethnic identities and loyalties as some sort of an atavistic residue to be erased with the march of modernity.[17] Similarly, ethnicity is seen as an impediment toward political integration and nationhood. My argument, on the contrary, is that when people of different origins come together in urban areas within a short period of time while maintaining ties with their home areas and constantly recreating in homogenous groups, their vision of life remains substantially unchanged.[18] The process of urbanization brings changes in cultural traditions. These changes, however, cannot happen at once. The feeling of belonging to an ethnic group may, in fact, be stronger in cities than it is in a homogeneous rural context. Ethnic affiliation is reinforced in urban areas because of the diversity found in these places. Such justification upholds my argument that urbanization, high levels of education, and high social status do not necessarily decrease ethnocentrism.

Ethnic identities provide meaning and content to the nation-state. Whatever point of view is adopted, the issue of ethnicity must be approached in a constructive way. Ethnic identities cannot be suppressed by the state. In acknowledging the role of ethnic identities, however, we must also be ready to grapple with these questions: Because of multi-ethnicities, what forms should the nation-state assume? How can we order the conflict of interests between the majority and the minority groups? What form should the concept of the common good assume in the midst of economic disparities that exist between ethnic groups? These questions could be answered insofar as we acknowledge that each ethnic group has a constructive role to play in the process of shaping political decisions. However, the strength of ethnicity is a two-edged sword. Ethnic identity, on one hand, when manipulated, can be the root cause of endless problems connected with disrespect of human rights and social justice. If appropriated properly, on the other hand, ethnic identities could be ingredients required for the realization of the ideal of civil society, participation, and political integration.

In most cases, ethnocentrism reveals itself in the form of resistance against the oppressive structure of the nation-state. It could also be said that the problem of ethnocentrism is closely related to the crisis of citizenship, political instability, economic insecurity, and the lack of an agreed-upon concept of the common good. While ethnicity cannot in itself form the basis of modern social organization, its potential in shaping social cohesion cannot be ignored. Such affirmation helps us to comprehend citizenship as a process that involves consensus-building between identities of ethnic groups while maintaining ethnic differences. The failure to recognize the influence of ethnic identity will continue to foment political instability, thereby exacerbating the situation of civil strife found in many countries. Ethnocentrism is not a result of primordial communal sentiments, sentiments that obstruct the unification of the nation-state; rather, it is a problem of incomplete political integration. Most of the African countries have failed to extend ethnic identity to the national identity.

It is often argued that economic insecurity makes autocratic leaders recruit men and women of their own ethnic groups into authoritative positions for the interest of their ethnic groups. Ethnic identities, taken from this perspective, generate a loss of national culture, a culture that could be enriched immensely by the absorption of different cultural identities. If ethnic identities are constructively appropriated they could become a national treasure. Ethnic identities are not evil in themselves as it has been portrayed by the forces of colonization and post-colonial politics. Ethnic identities become harmful when manipulated for self-interest. Henry Okullu makes the same claim saying that ethnic affiliation, as an extended family system, is a great asset in nation-building, especially when acting as a moral retaining influence and a means of security for its members.[19] It can be argued that an ethnic group as a larger family unit is an order of creation. A nation, some people would argue, is not an aggregate of individuals, but rather a unity of social groups and institutions, of which ethnic grouping is one. If such is true then ethnic groups are a foundation upon which a strong nation can be built. Building on the argument one could assert that it is unrealistic to think that a state can ignore ethnic identities without repercussions. My argument is that ethnic identities need not be destroyed; instead, what should be destroyed is the practice of manipulating them. Similarly it is a mistake to think that state affairs could be dictated from the viewpoint of one ethnic group.

The significance of ethnic identities has not diminished with the formation of nation-states for several reasons. First, family, clan, and ethnic group are still the essential structures of social relationships.[20] Second, one's identity is ethnic, not national. African leaders have done very little to convince their people that nationhood offers more benefits than ethnicity.[21] Third, African leaders have failed to define the relationship between an ethnic group and nation-state with respect to the common good. Fourth, African states have failed to appropriate inherited cultural traditions to help come to terms with the cultural realities of the times in order to emerge with a new vision for the future. Fifth, the approach of a nation-building has not attempted to find a way of welding together several ethnic groups into a large cohesive political community, a nation-state, intended to eliminate confusion and transfer ethnic loyalties to the larger political community. Sixth, there have been limited efforts made to formulate contextualized ideologies for contemporary Africa. Seventh, there have been no effective ways of dealing with traditional moral standards that seem to crumble in the wake of rapid socio-political change.[22] Eighth, most governments do not respect the freedom of the judiciary and the rule of law, which result into disregard for political morality and responsible leadership.

The emergence of ethno-political conflicts could be linked to the process of competing identities, loyalties, and interests. In many parts of Africa, ethnic loyalties have risen above other loyalties in contrast to the colonial era when there were limited incentives for this to occur. Today, loyalty to ethnic identity and interest could result into a quick promotion in one's status in places of work. If that is the case, then, how can Africa integrate ethnic identities, loyalties, and interests within the structure of the nation-state? To answer this question we have to acknowledge that

21

a leader has commitments not simply to general values and ideals but also to concrete people.[23] The process of decision-making and the kind of common good that one is committed to is heavily dependent on the loyalty of persons and groups that claim one's loyalty.[24] Loyalty can be influenced by interest group, cultural group, or religious group, which uses others as a ladder to acquire wealth and prestige. Conflicts in public life can therefore be looked at as conflicts between concrete commitments to various identities, loyalties, and interests. The analysis of Abner Cohen on the relationship between African cultures and modern politics in urban areas reveals that ethnic organizations camouflage their existence in public and its members adopt a low profile by attempting to fade into the general social landscape.[25] At the same time, however, its members must know about one another and should be able to recognize one another as co-members in order to coordinate their activities in the interests of the group and to avail themselves of the privileges of membership. They have to be visible to one another, but invisible as a group in public.

Maintaining a balance between competing identities, loyalties, and interests is possible by developing socio-political structures founded upon the principle of overlapping loyalties. This is the only possibility that can keep leaders from becoming persons who advocate the interests of a particular group. This project entails weighing competing loyalties and competing goods in order to act in a way that attends to their rightful claims.[26] The need to respect the diversity of ethnic identities is an important aspect of forming a cohesive political society. As such, the process of harmonizing competing loyalties could be achieved by maintaining a balance between the nation-state and ethnic communities. Such observation brings us to the need of understanding the relationship between ethnic identity and the common good.

Ethnic Identity and the Common Good

Ethnic identities shape the meaning of the common good. While ethnic sentiments may undercut the nationalistic approach, they may also be a force that enhances any sense of nationhood and common good.[27] Despite the call for national unity, the typical understanding of the common good remains limited to the framework of particular ethnic groups. Important issues such as how to form a nation based on political consensus and ethnic identities have not been extensively considered as expected since independence.

Involvement of an ethnic group in a super-structure like a nation-state should be understood from a perspective that enables each ethnic group to develop deliberative powers and a sense of purpose in search for the common good. In this process, accommodation of diverse social groups promotes a diversity of interests and enables each group to participate in the common structure laid down by consensus. The idea of political consensus can articulate new perspectives and preferences which will eventually enter into the balancing process by dissolving ethno-political competition and creating institutions that can guarantee equal citizenship, participation, and justice. This approach gives priority to those approaches that seep into the balancing process, affecting the shape of interest groups. Pluralism protects rights of individuals and groups by promoting political consensus based on consent. A balance of interests achieved by free bargaining between ethnic groups creates a comprehensive conception of the common good, and it should be regarded as a way of reducing destructive competition and hatred between ethnic groups.

The challenge for Eastern Africa countries is to formulate an inclusive concept of the common good based upon ethnic identities and political compromise. To develop such a paradigm does not mean that ethnic differences must be suppressed. The challenge we face is how to orient such identities toward an overlapping consensus that fosters the common good. Such a project entails developing a profound unity that respects ethnic diversity. It is not a unity that imposes uniformity, but a unity that cherishes participation and creativity in the interest of the common good.[28] This way of proceeding is valuable because the African understanding of the common good is still limited to the framework of the ethnic community. That is why city-dwellers are sensitive to the needs and interests centered on their village of origin and ethnic group. The place of birth and ethnic identities are seen as having influence over cities, despite the fact that cities are the seats of power and wealth. The understanding of the common good follows the same framework. The following two examples can illustrate this point. During his reign, Mobutu Sese Seko, the former President of the Democratic Republic of Congo, used state funds to construct an airport in his village, Gbadolite. In the same way, Felix Houphouet-Boigny, the former President of Côte d'Ivoire, built the state house and a basilica in his village, Yamoussoukro. These two examples show that ethnic identities remain the point of departure for the concept of common good that African nations intend to pursue.

Politicization of Ethnic Identities

Ethnic identities act as a pole around which group members are mobilized and effectively compete for state-controlled power and economic resources. Under the leadership of the predatory elite, members of the ethnic group are urged to form an organized political action-group in order to maximize their corporate political, economic, and social interests. Such a situation is sustained by the dynamics of the predatory politics that function to serve the interests of the ruling ethnic groups while the larger segment of society live in conditions of extreme poverty and marginalization.

Conflicts involving ethnic identities and loyalties have been summed up as those advocating interests of culturally distinct peoples, or clans in heterogeneous societies who are locked in rivalries over the access to power, and in which those concerned have certain regions as their stronghold and tend to follow the strategy of ethno-nationalism.[29] Political obsession with ethnic zones and ethnic discrimination is dismaying. Most of the political conflicts found in Eastern Africa today involve ethnic groups struggling for the control of their region (as it is the case in Sudan, Ethiopia, and Eritrea), or even struggling to control the entire country (e.g., Somalia, Rwanda, and Burundi). Such a phenomenon does not happen simply because of conservatism; rather, ethnic groups are also interest groups whose members share some common economic and political interests.[30] People do not kill one another merely because of the ethnic differences; rather, they kill each other when these differences promote unhealthy competition. The situation does not even become explosive until such a climate of social relationship is extended to the economic and political spheres.

Ethnic identities are not just a mere cultural identity limited to friendships, rituals, and marriages. They also play a significant role in informal relationships. A number of leaders, at the national level, allocate to their ethnic groups considerable state resources to maintain their political influence and control of the ethnic group concerned. Such leaders aim at maximizing their public support and access to resources in competition with rival politicians. Consequently the practice breeds destructive competition and conflict.

The competition for political power and limited economic resources has become intense in many countries. Political leaders, argues Solofo Randrianja, encourage the emergence of an ethno-nationalism in order to mobilize supporters.[31] This type of politicized ethnicity makes its appearance when nationalism extends its field of action to another level, from socio-cultural to that of politics. The progressive transformation of the Inkatha Movement in South Africa, which began as a cultural association into a political organization, is a good example. When ethnic groups are politicized, ethnic identities and loyalties move from the private sphere to the public sphere.

The tendency of politicizing ethnic groups tends to appeal to cultural identities for its effectiveness. In this project political leaders cooperate with cultural intermediaries in using cultural identity for political maneuvers. In this process, ethnic loyalties are reformulated to suit political strategies. Such leaders present themselves as representatives of the ethnic group while at the same time promoting their own interests. They combine carefully ethnic symbols with empty promises to manipulate the masses, especially where the colonial economy of predation, except in a few cases, has left the state as the main source of wealth and social advancement.[32] Politicization of ethnic identities appeals to the ethnic solidarity founded upon ties of blood-relationships as a means that can guarantee economic security. This approach takes the form of a conservative return to the grassroots of ethnic identities. It appeals to cultural symbols in order to construct a sense of allegiance, which makes it easier to mobilize people. Sometimes they use cultural slogans to arouse emotions of the people in order to make them accept what they do not even understand. That is to say interest groups competing for limited economic resources tend to invoke traditional sentiments to reinforce their appeal.[33] The success of political leaders in winning popular backing depends upon the trust which they inspire, and ultimately on their ability to obtain material benefits for their faction, in the form of government jobs or loans, a school or clinic, a road or electric supply. In this case we are dealing with a kind of patronage politics, with economic resources used as a political tool to enable the leaders to buy support for their policies.[34] Since political leadership may also appeal to ethnic identities to fulfill its ambitions, the practice of politicizing ethnic identities becomes one cause among many causes of ethno-political conflict.

By appealing to ethnic identities and loyalties political leaders urge people to keep allegiance to those who safeguard ethnic interests. The way of persuading people to support politicians tends to appeal to the traditional methodologies of supporting the traditional chiefs. Ordinary people feel that such politicians are about to restore the traditional political systems that guaranteed participation, solidarity, and security. However a number of political leaders, under the cover of African cultures, apply principles of manipulation and predation to serve their own interests. The consequence of using these methodologies is that ethnic groups are trained to acquire an attitude of concentrating on winning favors and fighting for the limited national resources. Their participation in public affairs is reduced to a game of advocating ethnic interests rather than building structures that can guarantee equal participation, justice, and development for all. Consequently people no longer see hard work as the source of economic success.

The introduction of multiparty politics in the 1990s started a competition that has shaped the context of struggle for political power among the political leaders and ethnic communities. Under the influence of ethnic politics voters do not appeal to the criteria of economic performance, health care services, education, and the common good. The important concern for them is enabling their members to control the state. The rationale used is to ensure that many from their ethnic group control government offices. Political leaders convince ethnic groups to believe that they rule the country on their behalf. The president is seen as an ethnic ruler. People believe that if one of theirs holds a high post, it is held in trust for the benefit of their ethnic community. Similarly, political parties have become ethnic parties slated for ethnic bargaining to acquire political power that would allow them to loot the state. It is from this perspective that a number of political parties promote ethnic politics, and regard the introduction of multiparty democracy as a way of decentralizing the state in favor of ethno-nationalism. Such practice creates mutual mistrust between ethnic groups. Those who belong to the less dominant ethnic groups feel left out and discriminated against by the system. In turn, they feel obliged to act, legally or illegally, to ensure their survival. The tendency of self-assertion emerging from different ethnic groups for survival is, in fact, the root cause of the widespread political instability.

Eastern Africa countries will prosper as modern nation-states insofar as there is an effort to decentralize ethnic politics. Reluctance to change will render the existing politics hostage to ethnocentric politics. The price of putting the tension of ethnic politics at the centre of African politics has become costly to the project of nation-building because such politics breed stereotypes that promote destructive attitudes between social groups underlined by exclusionary practices that develop without any rationale of the common good. Some ethnic groups, with peculiar identities and minority status, are often perceived as enemies to be destroyed just because their identities are different, and are perceived as dangerous competitors.

Ethnicity and Religion

Religion, as an agency of social interaction, is one of the most outstanding features of ethnicity. It contains a number of traditions considered to be a part of the ethnic community. These traditions play a significant role in the process of safeguarding ethnic identity. Religious ceremonies, for example, involve symbols which enhance the process of cultural identification. These ceremonies promote intra-ethnic social interaction situated at two levels, namely, formal and informal. In either case, religious activities provide an additional dimension of ethnic identification, which distinguishes one ethnic group from another. At the same time religion can manipulate ethnic identities, because religion is a product of culture. Such verification advances the claim that religion constitutes a significant variable deeply integrated into the overall complexity of cultural identity that provides a support system for ethnicity.

The function of religious institution is to propagate as well as safeguard traditions that shape the identity of the community, which, to a certain extent, brings together cultural traditions. The process of safeguarding traditions through religious institution helps to construct as well as maintain distinctiveness of an ethnic group. The preservation of the belief system is very effective in maintaining the separateness of an ethnic group that differentiates itself from other ethnic groups. With such a function one could argue that religion plays a crucial role in the process of formation, functioning, maintenance, and survival of an ethnic community. These characteristics uphold the claim that religion influences the concept of ethnicity.

Religion, as a foundation of group identity, provides a unified system of beliefs and practices that determines morality of the society. More than being what relates the individual to a higher being, it provides values that influence the way each individual relates to others. With these characteristics, religion becomes a significant variable in the way people see themselves, behave, and act. Such observations confirm that religion is an imperative to consider when studying the dynamics of ethnicity, politics, and citizenship. In determining people's identity, religion confers on the individual a sense of belonging. If religion provides a unified system of meaning, then it also provides the rationale for the organization of the society and the individual's place in it. Religion is more than a belief; it is also a system of action that functions to shape the value system and behavior.

By looking at the contemporary condition of Africa one could argue that the tendency of manipulating ethnic identities prevails also in Christian churches. The situation has robbed African churches of the ability to promote social justice.

According to David W. Waruta, most religious groups and denominations, closely scrutinized, are also ethnic in their composition and leadership.[35] Those that happen to be multi-ethnic with a national outlook are plagued with inter-ethnic conflicts. Ethnocentrism exists in churches as it does in the political sphere. In view of trying to understand the dynamics of this phenomenon one has to find out the real causes of the situation. As far as the history of African Christianity is concerned, this situation is linked to methods of evangelizing given ethnic groups in isolation, which produces a largely one ethnic denomination. In the process of maintaining their dominance, such ethnic groups tend to conduct their worship services in their ethnic languages, thus keeping out all others.[36]

From the perspective of administration, some ecclesiastical leaders are often appointed and assigned duties following the criterion of ethnic affiliation because a number of dioceses are created along ethnic lines.[37] Christian churches are lured by the clamor for each ethnic group to have its own bishop. Sometimes these arrangements are justified by language and cultural considerations.[38] It could be surprising if churches were not both a victim and accomplice of ethnocentrism. So far Christian leaders have been reticent about the ways in which they have been affected by ethnocentrism. Christian leaders tend to approach the challenge of ethnocentrism with extreme caution, creating ethnically encapsulated dioceses, and aligning with ethnically-oriented governments. Under such influence, it has been always possible to avoid appointing bishops who are ethnic outsiders, or who belong to unpopular minority ethnic groups.[39]

Christian teaching calls on its followers to promote a multi-ethnic community of an inclusive family of God built on faith, love, and hope. This teaching, however, has not yet become a reality because even churches have not remained untainted by ethnocentrism and partisan politics, and therefore they too have lost the ability to promote mutuality, social justice, and human rights. The challenge for the guardians of public morality who include churches is how to address this challenge in a constructive way. It does not suffice to know the problem; someone has to unveil evil practices in hope of soliciting appropriate action

29

otherwise they will torment us forever. The fear of addressing sensitive issues has crippled the growth of the continent. We are always afraid of telling the truth, and expect foreigners to do it on our behalf. Even the religious leaders who are expected to challenge the unjust social structures are indifferent. Christian churches have failed to play their prophetic role even in situations of severe human rights violations because they have taken sides by playing in the hands of partisan politics, thereby failing to transcend ethnic hegemony and discrimination.

The internal administration of churches has shown that their loyalty often lies with their ethnic groupings rather than with Christianity. In time of crisis, religious leaders, as political leaders, take refuge in their ethnic groups. A good example here is the genocide that occurred in Rwanda. In this event, Christians could not appeal to the Christian conscience to address the situation. Even those in positions of authority could not raise their conscience above the criterion of ethnicity. Christianity, for some, is like a coat that can be put on only when it is needed; when it is not, it lies forgotten in the wardrobe. This is the sign that Christianity is still on the periphery of the African way of life.

When Augustine Karekezi, a Rwandan Jesuit, was asked in an interview to link the role of the churches in Rwanda with what happened there in 1994 he said:

> My faith as a Christian has been affected seriously, in the sense that I cannot realize that such evil could happen in a country where so many people are Christians and where there are so many Catholics, over sixty five percent, with such influence in education. What have we been doing as Christians and as priests? How can we preach the love of God, the compassion of God, in this situation? All these questions emerge from an experience of the deep mystery of evil, evil that is so consistent and so strong that its power is prevailing.[40]

One may deceive oneself by saying that the conflict of Rwanda was a unique case, and that such experience does not exist elsewhere in the continent. The questions of Karekezi cannot be limited to the Christians of Rwanda. The experience of Rwanda should be taken as a typical example for many Christians of Africa. The experience of Rwanda reminds us that all Christians from Africa are called to ask themselves serious questions, especially the relevance of Christian faith in public life. We have to scrutinize very carefully the kind of evangelization found in Africa, especially the impact of preaching and celebration of the sacraments in social relationships. The question that can guide us in this engagement should be: How does Christian faith enrich the dynamics public life? There is no way we can avoid this question.

The challenge of the African churches is how to appeal to the Christian values to inform and transform social relationships. This is a serious challenge because churches are considered to be a part of the problem of ethnocentrism, and consequently they have also failed to stand above the situation. An expression that articulates the situation within the African churches says: the blood of ethnicity is thicker than the water of baptism. There are six points that uphold this assertion: first, for many years Christian churches have been using the structure of ethnicity for evangelization; second, churches have been reluctant to address the problem of ethnocentrism openly; third, bishops' pastoral letters have not yet succeeded in transforming public conscience because there is no active participation of Christians from the grassroots communities; fourth, an ethnic bias is also held by some ecclesiastical leaders; fifth, with regard to social problems, churches have failed to be self-critical; and sixth, there is no serious inter-religious collaboration intended to address socio-political issues because of religious competition.

The Rwandan holocaust underlines the artificiality of the kind of Christianity found in Africa. This is not a condemnation, but a matter of fair examination of conscience. There is no doubt that churches have failed to be the conscience of society in Africa. I do not, however, intend to argue that Christianity is automatically able to overcome the sinful nature of a human being. My observation is that a number of churches have failed to create even a minimum awareness of promoting mutual accommodation. This situation has been created by the fact that many churches have done very little to promote integral human development which includes awareness in social justice, human rights, common good, and political integration. The kind of religious knowledge emphasized in Eastern Africa, apparently, remains confined within the parameters of doctrinal dispute and religious competition.

Conclusion

In the preceding analysis we saw that ethnic identities become a blessing when they enrich social relationships. They can also become a curse when they become the source of political violence and social discrimination. In search for a balanced way to deal with ethnocentrism I would argue that Africa does not need to get rid of ethnic identities. Such an effort would not succeed because Africans, like all other peoples of the world, need to devise culturally informed modalities that can enable social groups to live together in a complementary relationship to each other. In view of implementing such modalities we ought to devise practical ways of promoting social cohesion through educational and cultural programs at the grassroots level so that ethnic identities and cultural diversities can be appreciated. Non-governmental organizations, including churches, can play a significant role in developing these programs. Inter-ethnic integration, tolerance, and mutuality could be promoted as political strategies. Such an initiative is urgently required because the situation in some countries is so bad that certain forms of ethnic discrimination are as dehumanizing as the apartheid system of the former South Africa. The problem can no longer be postponed; it has to be addressed as it will definitely not disappear.

Those who benefit from ethno-political competition tends to deny the fact that ethnocentrism exist in their countries. Such attitude has, to a certain extent, retarded the process of political transformation because it frustrates any effort geared to resolve problems related to socio-political organization. Similarly, because of the colonial background, we tend to blame the West for the problems caused by ourselves. My response toward this attitude is that the problem of ethnocentrism is real; and to simply wish it away, to condemn it without comprehending its roots and dynamics, or take no action to challenge it, only serves to strengthen it. The time has come to stop blaming foreigners, and instead take our responsibility seriously. We cannot lean on colonization forever as a paradigm of justifying our own shortcomings.

The search for long-term solutions to ethno-political competition and discrimination reveals that ill-founded methodologies tend to favor the model of exclusion founded upon ethnocentrism instead of equal citizenship. Such a model fosters rivalry between ethnic groups in gaining access to resources. The challenge of integrating cultural identities in the processes of political integration and democratization is closely related to the problematic concepts of nation-state, citizenship, and common good.

The process of cultural transformation entails transformation of the outdated traditions because they cannot confront emerging challenges of life. Every crisis requires a new solution because a problem arises as a result of sticking to the inherited value systems under new conditions that render such values inappropriate. In order to shift the centre around which people have tended to construct their selfhood and identity it is fitting to suggest other rallying points that can empower people to confront challenges of self-centeredness and exclusion. In order to succeed these paradigms must be promoted at all levels of social interaction and moral formation. Constructive changes will eventually emerge insofar as we are willing to overhaul inherited modalities of socio-political relationships as well as develop critical theories that can promote self-transformation.

Notes

[1] Stephen N. Ndegwa, "Citizenship and Ethnicity: An Examination of Two Transition Moments in Kenyan Politics," *American Political Science Review*, 91, 3 (June, 1997): 599-615, at 612. See also E. S. Atieno, "Hegemonic Enterprises and Instrumentalities of Survival: Ethnicity and Democracy in Kenya," in Bruce Berman, Dickson Eyoh, and Will Kymlicka, eds., *Ethnicity and Democracy in Africa* (London: James Currey Ltd, 2004), 167-183.

[2] Kipchumba Some, "How State Land Policy Shaped Conflict," *Daily Nation, Kenya* (February 10, 2008), 9.

[3] For further investigation on the background of ethnic land clashes, read Republic of Kenya, "The Report of the Select Committee to Investigate Ethnic Clashes in Western and Other Parts of Kenya," Nairobi: Government Printer, 1992); Leah Kariga, *Social Policy, Development, and Governance in Kenya* (Nairobi: Development Policy Management Forum, 2009), 10.

[4] Jeffrey Gettleman, "U.S. Envoy Calls Violence in Kenya 'Ethnic Cleansing,'" *The New York Times* (January 30, 2008): 1. See also "U.S. Envoy: Kenya Violence in Ethnic Cleansing," *http://www.mns.com/id/22908642* (Accessed on December 20, 2009); "Ethnic Cleansing in Kenya's Rift Valley," *http://www.cbc.ca/world/story/2008/01/30/kenya-envoy.html#skip300x250* (Accessed on February 20, 2008); Hussein S. Hafith, "Discrimination Still Rife in Kenya," *The Eastern Africa* (July 5-11, 2010): 7.

[5] Geoffrey Gettleman, "Signs in Kenya of Land Redrawn by Ethnicity," *The New York Times* (December 15, 2008): 1.

[6] Macharia Gaitho, "Will Kenya Continue to Exist as a Modern State?" *Daily Nation, Kenya* (February 5, 2008): 12.

[7] Relevant examples are given by Koigi wa Wamwere, *Negative Ethnicity: From Bias to Genocide* (New York: Seven Stories Press, 2003), 1-28.

[8] John Githongo, "Githongo on Kenyan Violence," *BBC World News*, *http://www.bbc.co.uk/2/hi/africa/7204987.stm* (Accessed on February 8, 2008).

[9] Editorial, "Kenya's Glimmer of Hope," *The New York Times* (February 22, 2008): 6.

[10] John Mbiti, *African Religions and Philosophy* (Oxford: Heinemann Educational Publishers, 1969), 102; Jean-François Bayart, *The State in Africa: The Politics of the Belly* (London: Longman, 1993), 50.

[11] John Lonsdale, "States and Social Process in Africa: A Historiography Survey," *African Studies Review*, 3, 2 (June-September, 1981): 139. I am not saying that modern African societies are to be organized in the same way. My argument is

that the operative force and validity of a particular model of social organization depends on the culture and historical background of the society concerned. As such, the structure of nation-state in Africa has not received support and commitment from the traditional models of political organization, governance, and leadership. It is a political structure imposed by predatory elites after independence.

[12] Josiah Royce, *The Philosophy of Loyalty* (New York: The McMillan Company, 1924), 52.

[13] Mwangi S. Kimenyi, *Ethnic Diversity, Liberty, and the State: The African Dilemma* (Boston: Edward Elgar, 1997), 45.

[14] David Lamb, *The Africans* (New York: Vintage Books, 1984), 9.

[15] Alfonce Shiundu, "Tribalism in State Offices," *Daily Nation, Kenya* (October 18, 2010): 68. The writer compiles many cases to demonstrate the raising trend of ethnic hiring and nepotism in public offices. He claims that many institutions, including public universities, have become ethnic institutions, instead of becoming national institutions.

[16] Heather J. Sharkey, "Arab Identity and Ideology in Sudan: The Politics of Language, Ethnicity, and Race," *African Affairs*, 107, 426 (December, 2007): 21-43, at 39.

[17] Mahmood Mamdani, *Citizen and Subject: Contemporary Africa and the Legacy of Late Colonialism* (New Jersey: Princeton University Press, 1996), 185.

[18] See, for example, the analysis of ethno-political interaction in the city of Nairobi, Kenya by Anthony O'Connor, *The African City* (London: Hutchinson University Library for Africa, 1983), 99-120.

[19] Henry Okullu, *Church and Politics in East Africa* (Nairobi: Uzima Press Limited, 1987), 45-46.

[20] Lamb, *The Africans*, 11.

[21] Ibid.

[22] Kwame Gyekye, *Tradition and Modernity: Philosophical Reflections on the African Experience* (New York: Oxford University Press, 1997), vii-xii.

[23] David Hollenbach, S.J., "Plural Loyalties and Moral Agency in Government," in John C. Haughey, ed., *Personal Values in Public Policy* (New York: Paulist Press, 1979), 77.

[24] Ibid.

[25] Abner Cohen, *The Politics of Elite Culture: Explorations in the Dramaturgy of Power in a Modern African Society* (Berkeley, California: University of California Press, 1981), 220.

[26] Ibid., 79.

[27] Henry Shue, Subsistence, *Affluence, and US Foreign Policy* (New Jersey: Princeton University Press, 1980), 144-152.

[28] Stanley Hauerwas, *Vision and Virtue* (Notre Dame, Indiana: Notre Dame University Press, 1974), 238.

[29] Ted T. Gurr, "People against States: Ethno-Political Conflict and the Changing World System," *International Studies Quarterly*, 38 (September, 1994): 347-377, at 355.

[30] For a similar thought, see Robert H. Bates, "Modernization, Ethnic Competition, and the Rationality of Politics in Contemporary Africa," in Donald Rothchild and V. A. Olorunsola, eds., *State Versus Ethnic Claims: African Policy Dilemmas* (Boulder, Colorado: Westview Press, 1983), 164-165.

[31] Solofo Randrianja, "Nationalism, Ethnicity, and Democracy," in Stephen Ellis, ed., *Africa Now: People, Policies, and Institutions* (London: James Currey and Heinemann, 1996), 31.

[32] Ibid., 32.

[33] William Tordoff, *Government and Politics in Africa* (Indianapolis: Indiana University Press, 1993), 86.

[34] Cohen, *The Politics of Elite Culture*, 79.

[35] David W. Waruta, "Tribalism as a Moral Problem in Contemporary Africa," in Jesse N. K. Mugambi and Anne Nasimiyu-Wasike, eds., *Moral and Ethical Issues in African Christianity* (Nairobi: Initiative Publishers, 1992), 112-130, at 127.

[36] Ibid., 128.

[37] See the findings of Mark Faulkner, "Evangelizing Gone Awry: The Church in Kenya has Fostered Tribalism it Now Deplores," *National Catholic Reporter* (February 22, 2008): 1-4.

[38] Ibid.

[39] Aylward Shorter, "The Curse of Ethnocentrism and the African Church," *Tangaza Occasional Papers*, No. 8, *Ethnicity*: *Blessing or Curse* (Nairobi: St. Paul Publications, 1999), 28-29.

[40] David Hollenbach, S.J., "Report from Rwanda: An Interview with Augustine Karekezi," *America* (December 7, 1996): 13-17, at 16.

3. Ethnic Diversity and Political Integration

Among the challenges encountered by contemporary Africa, one should include how to grapple with the diversity of ethnic identities in the process of molding cohesive political society. The subject of political integration has long been a crucial concern because of political disintegration.[1] It is unfortunate that the diversity of cultural identities has become a source of endless misunderstanding, discrimination, and conflict. The challenge derives from the fact that African countries are still tracing institutional paths of state-formation and nation-building. The effort of nation-building has ended-up promoting form without substance, thereby rendering the structure of the nation-state ineffective and superfluous. Such a situation has become a disturbing experience to the extent that Africa cannot develop without formulating appropriate solutions to the problems of socio-political organization, leadership, and governance.

The aim of this chapter, while focusing on the root causes of ethno-political competition and conflict, is to explore the challenges surrounding the process of political integration in the context of ethnic diversity. The argument that I intend to bring to the discussion, as an answer to the challenge of political instability, is that contemporary Africa needs politics that depend more upon public reason, dialogue, and consensus than inheritance, paternalism, and blood relationship. The study opens the inquiry by examining the dynamics of ethnic politics followed by relationship between corruption and ethnicity. Such an analysis intends to demonstrate that ethnocentrism is partially perpetuated by economic factors through the practice of corruption. The third part of the discussion attempts to justify the claim that democracy is an attitude of mind, and as such a serious promotion of democracy must, among many other things, concentrate on transforming the attitude and character, which effect social relationships. The fourth part evaluates a number of proposed possibilities intending to apply the principle of federalism to overcome ethnocentrism and conflict. The last two parts put an accent on the need of approaching cultural diversity as a means to enhance political integration.

The scope and methodology applied in the study focus on analysis, evaluation, and reflection on the prevailing ethno-political characteristics of self-centeredness, exclusion, competition, and conflict. They do not intend to provide readymade answers, but stimulate critical reflection. Clearly, an approach of this type is more helpful in the process of unveiling the root causes of the politics of disorder as well as formulates long-term solutions intended to transform attitude and character than those approaches that concentrate on chronological description of socio-political events.

The Politics of Ethnic Identity

Africa is the most fragmented continent in the world, probably because of ethnic diversity. There is no proof, however, that ethnic diversity is always associated with political disintegration and civil conflict. In a number of ways, apparently, ethnic diversity could be a source of discrimination, disintegration, and conflict. In the context of mutual hostilities between ethnic groups, there could be an increasing risk of secessionist movements and civil conflicts. Ethnic identity and diversity do not necessarily fuel the politics of domination and victimization of the minority ethnic groups. The condition of the inter-ethnic relationships depends on the political system, social interaction, and distribution of resources.

In some countries, it is ethnic identity that determines how to socialize, where to live, who to vote for in political leadership, and how to make choices in matters pertaining to public policy. Because of such background, the democratic movement has to account for ethnic identity in order to succeed. Ethnic identity, for many people, is a source of pride that guarantees protection of both political and economic interests. Until people find a way to integrate ethnic identity in political discourse, they will not be able to build a strong sense of citizenship, nationhood, and common good. A denial of this reality only benefits those who promote political disintegration for their own benefit. The rise of ethnic politics, after independence, could be linked to the secession movements searching for political autonomy due to the fear of marginalization for the minority groups.

The dynamics of ethnocentrism nourishes attitudes of intolerance, discrimination, and exclusion. These attitudes affect the framework of societal consensus, where individuals are coerced to conform to the prevailing sectarian thinking, prejudice, and politics of exclusion. The war against ethnic intolerance and exclusion remains elusive. Any effort geared to reveal the root cause of the failure would be appreciated, because it could provide insights that could be used to overcome the prevailing political instability. It is often argued that the fight for inadequate economic resources fuels ethnic rivalry. The situation is exacerbated when politics become a tool designed for the lawless scramble for limited resources, which is one in an atmosphere of scarcity and limited opportunities of advantage, through complex interplay between sectarian interest and identity difference. In many ways a number of the prevailing political leadership feed on ethnic prejudice, intolerance, and discrimination. Mutual exclusion is a situation widespread in places of work, learning, worship, and recreation. This practice produces discriminatory tendencies and corporate cultures that breed prejudice, marginalization, and violence.

Similarly, unjust wealth distribution has exacerbated ethnic divide as well as the practice of corruption. The ruling elite continue to accrue greater wealth, while destitution persists in the slums and rural areas. The divide between the rich and the poor has widened, thereby reinforcing conditions that generate divisive political extremism. There is no guarantee that progress towards democracy and governance could be made when ethnocentric mentalities prevail in the process of decision-making. The sign that the situation is not getting better is revealed through the phenomenon whereby an increasing number of intellectuals abandon the continent in search of economic opportunities abroad. They are forced to migrate because of continuing economic insecurity and unjust political systems that cause endless discontentment, injustice, and conflict. These variables have made Africa the most vulnerable continent in the world in terms of political instability, economic insecurity, and inter-ethnic conflict.

A critical examination of the dynamics of ethnicity, as a form of identity that influences socio-political relationships, could help us to understand how ethnic identity operates within political discourse, wealth distribution, politics of citizenship, formulation of national identity, and commitment toward community service. Such understanding would certainly facilitate any initiative intended to explore ways in which nation-states approach ethnic identity in view of promoting the ethics of inclusion in governance, multiculturalism, group representation, and resource distribution. Such examination reveals that identities are not fixed; rather, they are constantly shifting, negotiated, and contested. In the process they can be deconstructed, reconstructed, or manipulated depending on the prevailing conditions of life. Such a phenomenon is evident because ethnic identities are a consequence of socio-political change.

Creatively, ethnic diversity could be turned into a resource for political organization, especially as a resource that could be used to enrich democratic process and peace-building. Experience shows that there is evidence of politicized inter-ethnic rivalry and ethnic mobilization to acquire wealth as well as monopolize political power. It is through ethnic identification that competition for influence in the state and in the allocation of resources becomes apparent. A number of African governments have attempted to address the challenge through ethnic balancing in political appointments and wealth distribution. But the method does not always work because some ethnic communities tend to maintain their dominance at the expense of the impoverished ethnic communities.

A conversation about the influence of ethnic identity on political dynamics must necessarily explore social, political, and economic needs of the people concerned. The reason is that ethnicity by itself is not a problem; what is at stake is the way it is used for political and economic survival and concealment of exploitative practices as well as its tendency to marginalize and exclude others for the sake of self-interest. Examination of the politics of ethnic identity could possibly help us to answer the following questions: How can ethnic diversity contribute to the process of promoting democratic governance, strengthening of public institutions, and building a culture of accountability? Which innovative approaches and strategies can enhance inter-ethnic collaboration, mutual accommodation, and the common good? Which models of education can promote multiculturalism and inclusion in a multi-ethnic society? The following discussion attempts to answer these questions.

Ethnicity and Economic Incentive

Ethnocentrism has been perpetuated by economic incentive acquired through corruption. Such a practice has ended up destroying the sense of the common good and equal citizenship. In search for remedies I propose to examine the causes and the connection between ethnocentrism and corruption.[2] It is only through self-examination that effective solutions can be found to address the challenges of ethnocentrism, corruption, and conflict. Such an approach would simply highlight immaturity and inability to seriously challenge ourselves. In this evaluation I wish to concentrate on the relationship between ethnicity and corruption, while placing the phenomenon within its historical context. This approach attempts to relate corruption to ethnic politics, ethnocentrism, politics of the belly, lack of strong institutional control, and ethnic conflict. Another initiative revolves around the challenge of finding the most effective solution to end sectarian politics. In this struggle, people are called to work together to establish democratic governance based upon strict accountability and transparency. It must develop a people-centered society, empower people to exercise their sovereignty through civic education as well as carry out fundamental reforms in all public institutions. Such reforms would create the sense of moral responsibility and public commitment. Political leaders and civil servants are called to change their attitude, accept responsibility for the crime of looting their own people, and change their life-style and the way they render service to the public.

Corruption could be defined as an act in which the power of public office is used for personal gain. Economic corruption, political corruption, and moral corruption are closely interconnected. Corruption stands in fundamental contradiction to integrity, justice, and virtue. The practice of corruption is an evil

41

with the potential to multiply itself to the extent of affecting an entire society. It is like a group of evil people who protect each other for survival. In public institutions, it flourishes when officers in the civil service become rich at the expense of the poor.[3] Those who benefit from the practice of corruption do not want to be challenged on the ethical grounds of democratic governance, accountability, and transparency. They use state machinery to stop any initiative intending to challenge the evil of corruption.

Most of the African leaders do not have a good example to emulate. They simply came to occupy the seats vacated by the colonial rulers, enjoyed a similar status of predatory elites, and wished to hear nothing about democratic governance, accountability, and transparency.[4] Corruption is caused by irresponsible leadership, absence of popular participation in government, irrelevant institutions of governance, lack of accountability and transparency, politics without morality, weak judicial systems that appear to be foreign to the people's mentality, insecurity, and inadequate economic resources.[5] Similarly, because of the extended family system, leaders tend to identify closely with their relatives, clans, ethnic groups, and regions, and it is claimed that they have no alternative but to be corrupt to maintain this bond. A number of scholars justify the same claim, saying that African cultures of appreciation and hospitality encourage corrupt practices. Leaders are constantly pressured to help their relatives even when they are unable to do so. For those who hold office, it has been argued that society has a way of corrupting the public office holder because of the excessive demands and expectations placed on the resources of the individual.[6] The public office holder is expected to have an infinite reservoir of money as a base from which he is expected to dish out freely to assist his relatives and friends to escape the agony of poverty.

Extreme poverty has also been advanced to trace the origin of corruption. A number of political observers claim that people expect a public leader to be corrupt and wealthy. They look down on a leader who has not enriched himself at the expense of the state. They readily vote into power people they know can loot the state to enrich themselves and their respective ethnic communities.[7] Opposition politicians are simply waiting for their turn to eat through the practice of looting the state. Political leaders have become predators who take delight in exploiting the people they lead.

From the perspective of moral formation, corruption is caused by weak civic education, erosion of cultural consciousness, and lawlessness. The situation has created a belief that all politicians are corrupt, and unless the political institutions are fundamentally changed, no solution in the world can overcome corruption. Such initiative must be preceded by a change of attitude and mental framework toward the common good. We have to go beyond the politics of the belly[8] by transcending the claim that when a government official is dropped, people tend to say: they have taken food off his mouth. When a new one is appointed, they say: they have given him plenty to eat.[9] What is claimed here is reaffirmed in many parts of the continent of Africa. Any public job is seen as an opportunity to acquire wealth and prestige. Having acquired wealth through corruption, the civil servants, who are mostly regarded as the modern African chief, begin to distribute favors to their relatives, friends, and ethnic group. In East Africa, for example, the same practice is referred to when using the following saying: eat first. It is this cancer of looting the state with impunity that sustains African forms of corruption. In many ways corrupt leaders become the distributor of jobs, contracts, scholarships, and land. They receive bribes from multinational companies that loot their countries as well as import sub-standard goods.

A number of scholars argue that ethnicity plays an active role in the practice of corruption. The situation occurs when the politics of the belly uses ethnocentric ideology and clientelism. In search of political support members of the political elite tend to reward their relatives, friends, and ethnic groups. Consequently the distribution of public resources follows no just system, but the logic of self-preservation. African politics has been organized "to serve the interests of the political elite and their ethnic groups."[10] With every change of government, there are ethnic groups which fall into place for eating, thereby causing public discontent. This practice is properly examined in the book of Michela Wrong, *It's Our Turn to Eat*, where she examines the prevailing conditions that make corruption hard to eradicate.[11] In search for answers, she unveils two key questions: Why African leaders found it easy to reduce political discourse to the self-serving calculation of which ethnic groups get undeserved favors? When will the African leaders place the common good ahead of their ethnic community's self-interests? The analysis of Wrong, which is widely acclaimed as incisive, clearly reveals a tension between moral conscience and ethnic loyalty.

Another source of corruption that I propose to examine concerns the lack of ethical and religious values, both in political and economic activities. African leaders were brought up in a system of strict African ethical education and then introduced to Christian and Muslim moral values, but gradually they have become a disgrace to the continent. The input introduced by dominant religions has unfortunately become theoretical information that has nothing to do with social life. How religious spiritualities from the dominant religions have become so artificial and ineffective to Africa is a question that requires a critical examination. One hypothesis is that formal education and spiritualities of the dominant religions have failed to build on traditional African moral values, thereby failing to penetrate into the worldview and life style of the people. Another hypothesis is that since the state remains strictly secular, it follows that in the minds of the predatory elite morality has no place in politics and economics. Consequently the practice of looting the state is seen as an act of smartness on the part of those who do it.[12] For the younger generation, corruption is a normal phenomenon since it is done by everybody. For them, honesty is not a virtue, but a lack of courage to take care of oneself. These hypotheses have helped to institutionalize corruption. It does not pay to be a person of integrity in Africa. Merit is awarded to those who can give favors without considering the destruction it brings to the society morally. Corruption is linked to ethnicity when ethnic identities are used for justification. Those who promote ethnic interests see looting the state as a benevolent thing to do. Political leaders reinforce the ethnic cleavage in the process of looting the state because it protects them. Consequently, such a situation has brought a loss of integrity, self-confidence, and vision for the future. Corruption has also reinforced the culture of selfishness, looting, impunity, and irresponsibility. Corruption undermines any sense of dignity, moral accountability, and public good.

In order to challenge ethnocentrism, corruption, and exclusion, we have to empower the victims as well as reform political institutions. Such initiative could become a reality insofar the reforms are extended to the cultural and educational dynamics. The education given by families, communities, and formal schools should be based upon the values of the common good and service. The entire system of education requires radical overhaul and rethinking to bring about education for public service. In addition to that morality and religion must occupy the central position in education of the youth. Without a strong sense of moral responsibility people lose public conscience. We have to construct institutions that can reinforce the sense of public accountability, transparency, and civic education for the entire population.

It is through self-examination that effective solutions can be found to eradicate ethnocentrism, corruption, and conflict. Such an approach would highlight immaturity and inability to seriously criticize ourselves. The practice of corruption is so rife that it can only be fought collectively.[13] Corruption is much more than how everyday language defines it, for it is an attitude of mind before it enters the spheres of political discourse and wealth distribution.

Ethnicity and Federalism

Federalism could be defined as a system of political organization that puts emphasis on how power should be distributed between social groups and regions.[14] It focuses on preserving particular identities, loyalties, and interests. The principle of ethnic federalism refers to the coexistence of a set of political groupings that interact as autonomous entities, united in a common order, each with autonomy of its own. It is a kind of contractual agreement that represents a balance between centralism and devolution. The promotion of balance and compromise involves reciprocity and consent. Ethnic federation is strategically designed to enhance respect and management of political pluralism without accommodating authoritarian rule. If ethnic federation is not based on the culture of mutual accommodation, it promotes exclusion and secessionism, which eventually leads to the collapse of the federation as it occurred in the former Yugoslavia, Czechoslovakia, and Ethiopia, to mention but a few countries. Making reference to the African context, the paradigm of ethnic federation is rarely practiced with the aim of resolving ethnic conflicts.

From the perspective of functional arrangement, ethnic federation is not completely different from other types of federation. The fundamental purpose of ethnic federation is to achieve unity and understanding among the constituent groups, while at the same time preserving the identity and autonomy of each constituent. Other objectives envisioned by ethnic federalism include decentralization of the structures of governance, political devolution of power,[15] tolerance of ethnic diversity, self-actualization, and protection of the freedom of every citizen.[16]

A number of scholars, however, disagree whether federalism can overcome ethnicity-based challenges.[17] They claim that federalism could even intensify ethnic allegiance, division and rivalry, separation of regions, and corruption, thereby increasing the ethnic-based problems. Treating ethnic groups differently, through asymmetrical distribution of power, could raise the problem of inequality.[18] For others, socio-political division and tension can only be resolved by learning how to live together. Such a proposal becomes a reality insofar as we embrace the paradigms of pluralism, multiculturalism, tolerance, and participation as true subsets of democracy. This is the only way ethnic competition and conflict could be averted without causing damage to the cultural identity.

It appears that ethnic federalism cannot play a significant role in African political struggles for a number of reasons. First, neither a federal nor a unitary system is a solution to multi-culturally-based problems. Second, federalism cannot be a solution to multi-culturally-based problems because of manipulation by political leaders, self-interest, secession mentality, and inability to focus on the domestic causes related to predation, exploitation, and superiority complex. Third, ethnic federation could create inequality among ethnic groups and regions that leads to unhealthy competition. Fourth, modern leadership depends on the criteria of knowledge, competence, creativity, and responsibility, instead of blood relationship.

Correspondingly, the difficulty surrounding the principle of ethnic federalism is revealed in the following questions. First, since ethnic groups are different in terms of their size, population, and economic potential, who will occupy legislative and executive offices of the federal government? Second, should the federal government offices be dominated by ethnic groups that are big in size in terms of territory and population? Third, is the allocation of federal government offices based on the principle of proportional representation? John Coakley is similarly pessimistic about the possibility that ethnic federalism might reduce ethnic tensions.[19] He argues that ethnic federalism has been advocated as a conflict-regulating principle geared to promote a sense of security among members of the various groups, develop a sense of loyalty to the state, and eliminate fears of secession often raised within the framework of nation-state. A general survey shows that little has been achieved.

To sum up the import of the aforementioned questions, a number of political analysts argue that one of the major reasons for the breakdown of ethnic federation includes necessarily the lack of democratic governance.[20] The absence of democratic governance makes it difficult for ethnic groups to understand each others' perspective, interest, and aspiration. When ethnic interests overwhelm the good of the federation everyone tend to resort to ethnic aspirations, which include autonomy and secession. Because of the multi-ethnic character, there has been an agreement that there is no alternative to a federal system for countries like Ethiopia and Chad. Given the relative lack of cohesion and the persistence of ethnically-based misunderstandings since the introduction of the federal system, one could conclude that the experiment has not succeeded to overcome ethnic tensions. It is difficult to draw a conclusion that ethnicity-based federalism has been used as a fundamental organizing principle for a federal system of government. The pioneering experiment for applying the principle of ethnic federalism has been largely ignored in the growing literature on democracy and governance. Ethnic federalism, closely examined in terms of territorial decentralism to accommodate ethnic diversity, remains unpopular.

By looking at these difficulties we can ask ourselves the following question: Can we organize modern societies using the paradigm of blood ties? This question is crucial because it is ethically incorrect to ignore the import of democracy. My argument is that any form of leadership founded upon blood relationship is intrinsically problematic, because it is founded upon the attitude of self-interest and paternalism, instead of public reason and the common good where creativity, rational dialogue, community service, and freedom of choice prevail. Blood relationships cannot be justified rationally, thereby giving room for anarchy. Clearly, it is absurd to think of promoting ethnic federation as a paradigm that can sideline the movement of democracy. The point of contention is that the paradigm of ethnic federalism cannot function effectively in the modern world, because of the ethical pluralism enforced by urbanization, migration, and rationalization of the political debate. The modality of democracy is indispensable in the process of organizing contemporary societies because it acknowledges inclusiveness, participation, creativity, dialogue, freedom of choice, diversity, and devolution of power.

The process of democratization can strengthen social cohesion and institutional capacity to accommodate different social groups. Establishment of inclusive democracy requires a change of attitude and mutual accommodation. Such a framework could be built upon social relationships that bind a society together. The practice of democracy goes beyond blood relationships and ethnic affiliation on the condition that it advocates principles of tolerance, inclusion, and the common good. Such a ground must be revised constantly so that civic virtues can be under constant re-interpretation vis-à-vis the changing conditions of life. Democratic process, as a communicative process, is not simply a deliberation among citizens who share basic understandings, but rather a struggle among citizens to have their identities recognized by others. It is a process that requires participants to listen to all forms of expression and proposal that aim to cooperate so as to attain a solution that is inclusive and appropriate for addressing collective problems.[21] Such a norm of inclusion supports the claim that no culture can claim to be better than others.

There is no way we can live peacefully without taking seriously the ideals of democracy. We cannot organize ourselves competitively and effectively in the modern world following the principle of blood relationship. Contemporary Africa is therefore called to organize itself in terms of post-ancestral paradigms; otherwise we will not be able to live together. Contemporary Africa has greatly changed, and as such new mutations have taken place. Under these conditions I wish to argue that we can no longer cling to the ancestral paradigms without introducing into them some sort of innovation. It is imperative to invent new paradigms that can meet the challenges of the modern world. The future depends on such creativity, not on a wholesale return to the world of the ancestors. The past can only provide inspiration that could be used as a starting point.

Cultural Diversity and Political Integration

Politics of identity grapples with the challenge to respect cultural diversity. Such initiative has emerged with a view to combat the attitude of exclusion revealed through ethnocentrism and marginalization. It could be argued that this approach attempts to expand the sphere of civil society. The recognition of diverse cultural identities is indispensable in the process of organizing human society because no one would like to be overshadowed. The challenge of political disorder and inequality revolves around cultural identity and group interest. The demand for recognition entails respect for every person. Such a demand represents an effort to acknowledge difference, diversity, and the need of inclusion.

Consideration of the politics of identity and inclusion brings us to the question of equal citizenship and multiculturalism. In the search for appropriate political organization, the framework of democracy provides a space for different identities to interact as well as respect one another to enrich the concept of the common good. The tendency of compelling all citizens with different identities to conform to a unitary ideal does not accommodate differences and tends to marginalize minority groups. Such a claim reminds us that equal opportunity for all becomes a reality when there is an attitude of acknowledging diverse identities within the society. It opens the door toward accommodation of different identities. The diversity of cultural identities does not necessarily negate unitary models of citizenship, loyalty, and mutuality. An inclusive methodology of building a political community founded upon collective identity must be open to diversity so as to avoid ethnic hegemony. In order to form an ordered society that respects inclusion and equality, the following conditions must be respected: first, organize a legal constitution that reflects different psycho-social realities operating in terms of political, cultural, and religious identities; second, build a platform to which all citizens can feel attached in order to strengthen the sense of common citizenship and nationhood; third, construct a collective identity with a possibility of providing room for each social group to exercise the right of self-determination; and fourth, construct institutions founded upon principles of diversity, inclusion, and the common good. Such a collective organization can overcome the urge of compelling people to conform to one model that is possibly derived from dominant social groups. The convergence of identities could be achieved through public debate and free interaction in accordance to the principles of social interdependence and political compromise.

The challenge of pluralism reminds us that the recognition of cultural, political, and religious difference poses a salient question to the study of the ethics of multiculturalism, ethnic politics, and political integration.[22] The post-modern tendency of appealing to universal moral norms is limited. We continue to use many of the key expressions, but we have largely lost their comprehension. Such a sociological datum renders the discourse on democracy and universal moral norms abstract. Such sentiments likewise inspire religious interpretations of morality which contends that any attempt to establish a universal ethic grounded in human nature is unrealistic because it takes lightly the historical import. Religious ethics fails to appreciate the fact that there is no universal morality, but that we live in a fragmented world of moralities. A number of ethnocentric perceptions are, to a certain extent, confined to an intramural conversation that makes them sectarian. In addressing the problematic status of ethnic politics, we have to consider the scope and limit of any political theory as it applies to a wide range of socio-ethical issues.

The aforementioned situation suggests that there is a need to construct a concept of democracy founded upon the principle of diversity, which aims at developing public attitudes and political structures that can yield a point of view acceptable to all. Such a perspective involves a process of moral struggle intended to achieve an inclusive political sphere. Accordingly, if we want to construct inclusive democracy, we must take into account processes of historicization and localization of moral norms. How can we construct a concept of democracy, which is contextual, inclusive, and accepted by all? In other words, can we envision a concept of democracy based upon a historicized justification that truly serves as an overlapping consensus of divergent conceptions of the good? Particular conditions of life and cultural identities, as related to the process of historicization, stand as necessary factors that justify the validity of democratic ideals. Such a claim attests clearly that processes of historical consciousness of every group of people count as factors that guarantee concretization of democracy. If this is true of all cultures, then when dealing with the issue of common morality, we must maintain the balance between particularity and universality.

The interaction between cultures justifies the claim that there is an intercultural communication that results in a dimension of common morality. Considering the concentric cycles of morality, universality should be attained as a communion of particular entities. It is therefore unrealistic to ignore the role of cultural traditions and value systems in search of a reasonable way to establish an ordered society. If an ethical principle separates itself from historical experiences, it will be without historical justification. Every ethical principle is embedded in a complex web of ideas that arise from social relationships. An ethical principle cannot be neutral. It is impossible to reach judgment about the truth or falsity of ideas without "relying on other ideas that form that part of the web. There are no first principles that have no presuppositions."[23] Following the framework of this argument, we can conclude that we must take into account concepts of difference, particularity, and diversity because they derive from cultural identity.

What we have seen suggests that the operative force of moral norms governing the process of democratization is inseparable from the cultural dynamics. Any theory focused on democracy cannot be justified unless it is intimately linked with the value system of a particular culture. Such a demand opens the door through which we can appreciate the role of culture in the process of political transformation. It is a process that justifies the claim that democratic ideals cannot be actualized unless we identify them with particular communities, cultures, and institutions. We must acknowledge that moral norms are contextual, differ from one community to another, and change with time.

Outdated cultural traditions obstruct rational dialogue and structural innovation. Such is the case when cultural fundamentalism underestimates the common dimension shared between cultures. The inward-looking tendency within cultures promotes the attitude of exclusion between ethnic groups in the form of ethnocentrism. Such a situation renders political integration impossible. The attitude of exclusion results in repression and marginalization. A balanced approach to cultural identity promotes a humanist model underlying values of self-determination, cross-cultural collaboration, and inclusion.

Cultural diversity should be viewed as a possibility to be realized, not a problem to overcome.[24] There is no need to fear it, for it is a part of socio-political organization. What we have to do is to struggle with the challenge of maintaining continuity with the past and dialogue between cultures. When it comes to supporting multiculturalism in terms of recognition and accommodation, Howland T. Sanks argues that it can be achieved insofar as we conceive the relationship between past cultural expressions and the diverse cultural expressions currently possible as one of cultural dialogue.[25] Such a dialogical relationship would recognize the originality of each culture, the inadequacy of each, and the consequent need for mutual criticism, openness, and collaboration. In order to encounter the other, one has to be oneself and, at the same time, one should be able to find a point of meeting and understanding the other. Through this dialogue, one not only learns to understand the other, but acquires also a deeper understanding of oneself. We ought to acknowledge that a moral agent, attempting to respond to the challenges of life, is fashioned by cultural narratives. As such, the process of democratization must be seen as a way of responding to different cultural conditions. The promotion of democracy involves a change of each one's attitude toward other cultures, and developing new structures of mutual exchange. Such an interaction provokes deeper insights that could enhance dialogue and collaboration in addressing the challenge of organizing the political sphere.

A democratic discourse cannot be justified by an abstract formalism of a non-historical ideal. It must be situated within historical experiences in which people are nurtured. As such, efforts geared to promote democracy should be more than a mere application of a set of moral principles legalized by a particular convention. If agents of human rights and democracy ignore the influence of local cultures, then the rhetoric of democratization will be reduced to a mere body of information that cannot produce practical impact. To make the issue of democracy a reality, we must listen to all cultures without condoning weaknesses embedded within them. This process is essential because transformation of moral systems comes from within cultures. It is through cultures that the transformation of people's attitudes, character, and behavior become possible.

Acknowledgement of particularity in terms of cultural identities is not an enterprise that can threaten the dimension of universality. Instead, it strengthens the dimension of distinctiveness as well as unity in plurality. Francis B. Nyamnjoh sums up the importance of respecting cultural diversity in promoting democracy, saying that inclusive democracy calls for scrutiny of the importance of cultural identity in the lives of individuals and groups.[26] This argument challenges reductionist views of democracy, and acknowledges the fact that democracy may take different forms, above all by being constructed differently in different societies, informed by history, culture, and economic factors. The liberal democratic rhetoric of rights must listen to, and take on board, creative responses informed by cultural traditions, historical experiences, and socio-economic circumstances. Realization of democratic ideals is an unending process subjected to renegotiation with changing conditions of life and growing claims advanced by individuals and groups for mutual recognition. The claim put forward by Nyamnjoh is crucial because the ethics of universality tends to overlook the concept of particularity. By so doing one depletes local engagement and creativity, which emerge from particularity. Over-emphasis on universality could overshadow principles of subsidiarity and localization altogether.

Difference and identity have become controversial factors surrounding the process of democratization. Political movements are deeply influenced by cultural identities, and as such the politics of identity have become avenues of self-expression and self-assertion in the public sphere. It is not easy to accommodate the diversity of identities and conflict of interests between individuals and groups. In the modern world, because of global interaction and migration, there is no society that is going to be homogenous in culture and religion. Nevertheless, there is nothing to fear; people with different perceptions of the good can live together harmoniously. Such a possibility supports the claim of multiculturalism, which is about living in culturally, religiously, and ethnically diverse society.

We are no longer able to speak of one cultural tradition as being superior to others. Cultural fundamentalism has no room in the modern world. Claims of superior and inferior cultures, or of true and untrue religions are irrelevant and raise unnecessary competition. In the modern world, we ought to talk of different traditions as partners in the process of building a democratic culture. The art of social organization, remarks Ian S. Markham, requires mutual enrichment, which involves both separateness and engagement. Instead of a "unity culture where one language, one religion, one history, and one set of images dominates, we need diverse culture where different languages, many religions, several narratives, and images coexist in stimulating alternative thinking."[27] Let us welcome the diversity of cultural traditions, different religious options, and variety of perspectives in the way we think. Instead of the learning centers and media promulgating one way of seeing things, let different traditions articulate different ways. Each community needs a space to nurture its identity. Mutual enrichment, arising from different cultures, nourishes alternative thinking and exploration of truth.

The politics of difference acknowledges diversity, inclusion, and particularity of cultural identities. Such understanding advocates a possibility for diverse cultural groups with different backgrounds to live together with an agreed-upon path of pursuing shared objectives. This approach is an attempt to overcome ethnocentrism, prejudice, exclusion, and marginalization, which tend to obstruct possibilities of organizing a society that upholds equality. As opposed to conformity, multiculturalism sponsors the politics of pluralism for the sake of the common good. In support of this idea, Iris Marion Young argues persuasively that "a good society does not eliminate group difference; rather, it upholds equality among culturally differentiated groups who mutually respect and affirm one another in their differences."[28] This way of thinking presents a possibility of cross-cultural interaction and sharing of common experience in view of promoting values that can sustain mutuality.

Pluralism forms a paradigm that accommodates divergence in value systems, cultural traditions, and practices. Pluralism advocates the freedom of choice individuals enjoy as they decide how to come together to pursue their common interests. Just as the marketplace emphasizes open competition, with the expectation that what is good will prevail over a long period of time, "pluralism emphasizes constant negotiation, with the expectation that the consent of all will be won in the long-run."[29] It is not true that accepting pluralism will cause misunderstandings as often argued by proponents of conformity and status quo. Contextualized, inclusive, participative, communicative, and progressive forms of democracy recognize that political dialogue approaches collective problems by acknowledging that plurality of perspectives, interests, and sovereignties exist. Robert Dahl upholds the same argument saying that "instead of a single center of sovereign power there must be multiple centers of power, none of which can be wholly sovereign."[30] Although the only legitimate sovereign is the people, even the people ought never to be absolute sovereign. Such understanding requires an extension of shared understandings about political community.

Politics of identity, multiculturalism, and pluralism challenge ethnic hegemony, conformity, and marginalization. It advocates variables of diversity, identity, and particularity as valuable forms of self-discovery and self-actualization. Such understanding cherishes the role of cultural traditions to facilitate mutual respect and collaboration. This approach denounces hegemonic culture to which minority cultures are coerced to conform. Respecting diversity safeguards fundamental rights of individuals and groups, and thereby induces readiness for cross-cultural engagement, which rejects all forms of cultural hegemony and cultural imperialism.[31] Democratic principles and the politics of diversity transcend ethnocentrism by cultivating institutional inventiveness and flexibility which result in public recognition of cultural diversity. Multiculturalism recognizes cultures as life forms of self-awareness and self-actualization where meaning is structured along both empirical and transcendental experiences.

The democratization process requires people to respect all cultures as a means to overcome mutual suspicion and exclusion. We have to learn to appreciate each other. We cannot escape the fact that we live in societies peopled by a vast number of social groups, diverse experiences, and traditions. Diversity has increased as a result of migration, and it is compounded by the fact that we live in an era of global interaction that makes us aware of the differences within our own communities and around the world.

The politics of identity forms a feature of the multicultural world in which we live, and challenges hegemonic tendencies. It advocates inclusion by broadening the art of political organization and inter-ethnic dialogue. It is a justifiable means of overcoming ethnic hegemony since it invites all social groups to the table of dialogue, consensus-building, and planning for the sake of the common good. In the processes of promoting civic virtues, cross-cultural and multicultural paradigms must be considered. It is a process of making sure that everybody is considered and invited to contribute to the cause of the common good. Such a consideration, as we have seen earlier, is crucial because common morality derives from particularity and diversity. It is an inclusive framework geared to appreciate cultural difference, diversity, and self-determination. Sentiments geared to promote forcefully cultural and religious traditions founded upon sectarian interests, as seen among conservatives, will not enrich the concept of the common good.

The fear that too much attention to cultural particularity will be divisive is unrealistic. Particular identities do not cause harm in themselves; instead, they are a part of exercising one's individual freedom and potentiality within a given group of people. Respect for particular identities is essential because each person is expected to benefit from the experience of engagement with other cultures as a means of enriching one's own culture. The fact is that we are already in a divided world; and if we want to construct ordered societies, then we must be in dialogue with cultural differences. It is therefore worthwhile to note that the root cause of political disorder ravaging African countries emerges from the inability to integrate ethnic identities and loyalties into the political process.

Taking Democracy Seriously
A democratic system provides an inclusive sphere where balancing of power, ordering of interests, and participation become a reality. The advantage of democracy is that it establishes a common moral understanding that allows people to collaborate in addressing social challenges and organizing political life. It seeks to establish harmony without destroying identities, loyalties, and a variety of inputs coming from different institutions. However, the challenge of building a democratic culture is how to organize incompatible perceptions of life in such a way that the diversity within the community remains preserved. The lack of a common universe of discourse is caused by plurality of experiences. As a response, accordingly, John Courtney Murray and Reinhold Niebuhr address the challenge of diversity by proposing basic guidelines in the process of building a political society.[32] They argue that public dialogue facilitates constructive conversations. This process lays the foundation for public discourse intended to transform brute facts into arguable claims. Through mutual reflection, this

57

approach focuses on the areas of common interest. This process plays the role of combining opinions in order to establish priorities that can establish consensus. A consensus attained in this way recognizes differences between interest groups and individuals who hold different views with regard to the good life.

The political thought of Murray and Niebuhr on democracy illuminates considerably the task of establishing a comprehensible framework for the common good in a pluralist society. Niebuhr presents a balanced framework of organizing complex society by asserting that human inclination to injustice makes democracy necessary.[33] For him, democracy is a valuable framework for organizing society politically that does justice to the spiritual stature and social character of human existence. The tension between individual and community is inevitable because individuals and groups seek to guard their interests in terms of power and privilege. In search of a lasting solution to this situation, democracy becomes indispensable. The horizon of democracy goes beyond political, religious, and cultural tendencies of exclusion on the ground that it seeks to embrace all spheres of experience, identity, and interest. We cannot attain socio-political cohesion by imposing on everybody a single vision of life arising from a single group of people.

The political thought of Niebuhr presents insights that seem to be crucial in organizing a political society. He claims that neither liberalism nor collectivism has succeeded in overcoming social injustice. One institution, on its own, cannot resolve the conflict of interests because each group in society seeks to guard its identity, power, and privilege. On the role of religion in the public sphere, he claims that religious vision alone cannot overcome the conflict of interest and injustice because religions tend to abstract the consciousness of an individual from social realities and focus too narrowly on the meaning of life, search for happiness, and tend to withdraw the believer from social responsibility which finally limit the individual.[34] Similarly, aggressive secularism could be destructive because it operates as though it has readymade answers to all problems of political life. The dream of an absolute secularism is dangerous at best because it brings about spiritual vacuum and totalitarianism.

A democratic system provides an inclusive sphere where balancing of power, ordering of loyalties, and participation become a reality. The advantage of democracy is that it establishes a common moral understanding that allows people to collaborate in addressing social problems. It seeks to establish harmony without destroying identities, loyalties, and a variety of valuable experiences coming from different institutions. Nevertheless the challenge of building a democratic culture is how to organize incompatible perceptions of life in such a way that the diversity within the community remains preserved. The lack of a common universe of discourse is caused by plurality of experiences. As a response, Murray addresses the challenge of diversity by proposing basic guidelines in building cohesive political society. He argues that public dialogue facilitates constructive conversations. The horizon of such process lays the foundation for public discourse intended to transform brute facts into arguable claims. It is through mutual reflection that this approach focuses on the areas of common interest. This process plays the role of combining opinions in order to establish priorities that can establish consensus. A consensus attained in this way recognizes differences between interest groups and individuals who hold different views with regard to the good life.

The convergence of identities, loyalties, and interests occurs through the common vision that seeks to improve the quality of life for all. Such a vision finds its locus within the framework of the common good that could be attained without uniformity of religious beliefs and cultural traditions. What is required is the shared understanding of the common good. In this framework the political consensus furnishes a common universe of discourse through which public issues are intelligibly stated and argued.[35] Such a ground of collaboration has to be established in a way that experiences arising from various institutions and cultures are taken seriously by creating a ground upon which all those members of the community who have ideas to contribute are allowed to do so. The procedures of building political consensus must be public so that public decisions become the work of the whole community. No single formulation will be able to capture the whole meaning arising from all dimensions of life. It is only through overlapping consensus that people from diverse religions and cultures reach agreement on the standards of justice for the institutions that structure their lives together. They discover within their "particular traditions adequate grounds for affirming a set of basic moral principles that persons from other traditions can also affirm for their own reasons."[36] The consensus-building process reflects a union of minds attained through widespread agreement, shared deliberation governed by norms of rational inquiry,[37] interaction between private and public spheres of justice served by a network of reciprocity,[38] and mutual respect.[39] This understanding makes the framework of the common good an overlapping principle able to bring people together with an ability to respect differences.

Democracy is a means to build ordered social life and the common good, where human rights are respected and the establishment of social justice and quality of life become the object to pursue. Democratic ideals can be realized insofar as there are institutions capable of guaranteeing and safeguarding the sovereignty of peoples. In such a framework, the state is engaged in sustaining conditions that promote development for all citizens. Such framework guarantees institutionalization of fundamental rights, political participation, and social justice. The aforementioned understanding shows that Africa is called to develop the spirit of republicanism, the spirit of respect for the rule of law, fairness, and common good in order to establish a stable social organization. Democratic values could be promoted when there is authentic mental metamorphosis, cultural transformation, and civic education within the multicultural framework intended to challenge the attitude of exclusion.

A number of African scholars argue that democracy in indigenous African societies was both individual and collective, and involved a great deal of negotiation and compromise by individuals and communities to which they belonged at all levels of socio-political interaction. The way forward should emerge from the process of recognizing creative ways in which people merge traditions with exogenous influences to create realities not reducible to either but enriched by both. Thus, approaches that expect to unearth readymade ethical principles from the past, or restore the administrative models applied by African ancestors could end-up being misguided, because these principles cannot be applied directly to the prevailing conditions of the present time. We have to be very careful with all the ongoing rhetoric that tends to limit African political thought to the past. We must be courageous enough to invent paradigms that can be effective and transformative in the modern world.

For Africa, the debate on political integration must include a serious discussion with a focus on the necessity of promoting democratic accountability and good governance. We have to take up the challenge seriously by democratizing public institutions and programs of moral formation. For political integration to become a reality, the democratically decentralized powers must be in the hands of the majority instead of the predatory elite.

Conclusion

A return to the world of the ancestors cannot be an adequate solution to the problems of the modern world. The administrative paradigms practiced by ancestors cannot be applied in wholesale fashion to the modern world because the conditions of life have significantly changed. We can only refer to the past for inspiration, not for direct application in organizing contemporary political life. We can conclude this chapter by saying that the challenges we encounter today include inability to change by failing to make a shift from ethnic politics characterized by the attitude of self-centeredness and exclusion. If we cannot make a shift from these paradigms, then the political future of the continent will remain uncertain.

In order to make political integration possible there must be mechanisms intended to make people agents of change. Development cannot be imported from abroad as a readymade product; it has to be experienced as participation in the process of building it. It is about being self-responsible and engaged in the process whereby the dream of self-realization comes into being. Similarly, democracy comes from the inside of the person through the process of being willing to engage others in building the framework of the common good. Democracy that can empower people is built progressively; it cannot be imported from abroad as a readymade product for consumption. It is a capacity-building process sustained by programs of moral formation and political participation. The art of political organization is a process of cultural transformation, liberation of one's mindset, and self-determination. The formation of a cohesive society is not a process of reinforcing uniformity, but rather a process of self-actualization engaged in self-transformation and mutual accommodation.

Notes

[1] The background of the problem of political integration for Africa is clearly articulated in the overview of Rene N'Guettia Kouassi, "The Itinerary of the African Integration," *African Integration Review*, 1, 2 (July, 2007): 1-22. The expression "political integration" will be used throughout this work, meaning political cohesion, mutuality, and peaceful coexistence between ethnic communities.

[2] For further elaboration on how the practice of corruption is a drawback to the African development, see the findings of Kevin Mwachiro, "Kenya Corruption Costs Government Dearly," *http://www.bbc.c.uk/news/world-africa-11913876* (Accessed on December 3, 2010). He claims that the Kenyan government is said to be losing about four billion dollars, which is nearly one-third of the national budget, to corruption every year. In this process individuals take huge sums of money set aside for development projects.

[3] Joseph Warioba, "The Report of the Warioba Commission on Corruption," *Business Times, Tanzania* (June 27, 1997): i – xxxii, at iii.

[4] John Mary Waliggo, "Corruption and Bribery: An African Problem?" *http://www.fluc.org/sap/* (Accessed on May 10, 2010).

[5] Africa's change from democratic governance to oppressive one-party system, military regimes, and coalition governments is primarily due to the desire of the political leaders to acquire easy access to resources without being accountable to the people.

[6] Aquiline Tarimo, S.J., "The Extended Family and the Cycle of Poverty," *African Christian Studies*, 20, 2 (June, 2004): 5-32, at 15.

[7] Corruption, from my viewpoint, will be eradicated when the financial incentive is completely removed from the political sphere. Such initiative must direct wealth toward wealth-creators. Such initiative will discourage those who enter politics for the purpose of generating wealth for themselves instead of service. Boldly stated, let there be no money in the sphere of politics, and everything will be alright in the spheres of social justice and economic development.

[8] The politics of the belly is also known as prebendal politics, a notion used in the book of R. Joseph, *Democracy and Prebendal Politics in Nigeria: The Rise and Fall of the Second Republic* (Cambridge: Cambridge University Press, 1987).

[9] Jean François Bayart, *L'Etat en Africa: La Politique du Ventre* (Paris: Fayard, 1989), 10.

[10] Waliggo, "Corruption and Bribery: An African Problem?" 16.

[11] Michela Wrong, *It's Our Turn to Eat: The Story of a Kenyan Whistle-Blower* (New York: HarperCollins Publishers, 2009).

[12] Ibid., 18.

[13] Corruption is a widespread practice in all institutions, including Christian churches. See, for example, the report on the claims of bribery practiced by bishops vying for the top post accused of dishing out cash to buy voters ahead of the Anglican Church of Kenya Elections in April, 2009. The report is compiled by Jonathan Manyindo and Peter Nge'etich, "Bribe Claims Ahead of ACK Poll," *Daily Nation, Kenya* (April, 21, 2009): 4.

[14] Bakris Herman, *Federalism and the Role of the State* (Toronto: Toronto University Press, 1987), 5.

[15] Jaramogi Oginga Odinga, *Not Yet Uhuru: An Autobiography of Oginga Odinga* (London: Heinemann Educational Books, 1967, 294.

[16] Raymond Rosenfield, ed., *The Challenges of Federalism: USA, USSR, and Ukraine* (Kyiv: National Academy of Public Administration Office of the President of Ukraine, 2008); Jenna Bednar, eds., *A Political Theory of Federalism* (London: Stanford Institute of International Studies, 1999), 17.

[17] For further analysis, see the arguments of Dean E. McHenry, Jr., "Federalism in Africa: Is It a Solution to, or a Cause of Ethnic Problems?"

http://www.federo.com/pages/federalisminAfrica.html#1
(Accessed on May 5, 2010).
[18] William Tordoff, *Government and Politics in Africa* (Indianapolis: Indiana University Press, 1984), 72-73.
[19] John Coakley, ed., *The Territorial Management of Ethnic Conflict* (London: Frank Cass, 1993), 19. Other scholars who hold the same position include Davis S. Rufus, *The Federal Principle* (Berkeley, California: University of California Press, 1978), 211-212; Roberta McKown, "Federalism in Africa," in C. Loyd Brown-John, ed., *Centralizing and Decentralizing Trends in Federal States* (Lanham, Maryland: University Press of America, 1988), 298; Donald Rothchild, *Managing Ethnic Conflict in Africa* (Washington, D.C.: Brookings Institution Press, 1997), 57; Vincent Maphai, "Liberal Democracy and Ethnic Conflict in South Africa," in Harvey Glickman, ed., *Ethnic Conflict and Democratization in Africa* (Atlanta: The African Studies Association Press, 1995), 106.
[20] Among such scholars see, for example, Claude Ake, *Democracy and Development in Africa* (Washington, D.C.: The Brookings Institution, 1996); John W. Harberson, Donald Rothchild, and Naomi Chazan, eds., *Civil Society and State in Africa* (Boulder, Colorado: Lynne Rienner Publishers, 1994); Seyla Benhabib, *Democracy and Difference* (New Jersey: Princeton University Press, 1996).
[21] Iris Marion Young, *Inclusion and Democracy* (Oxford: Oxford University Press, 1996), 80.
[22] Essays that present an exemplary data are found in the work compiled by Sverker Gustavsson and Leif Lewin, eds., *The Future of the Nation-State: Essays on Cultural Pluralism and Political Integration* (New York: Routledge, 1996).
[23] David Hollenbach, S.J., "Religion and Political Life," *Theological Studies*, 52, 1 (March, 1991): 87-106, at 103.
[24] Howland T. Sanks, *Salt, Leaven, and Light: The Community Called Church* (New York: Crossroad, 1992), 202.
[25] Ibid.
[26] Francis B. Nyamnjoh, "Reconciling the Rhetoric of Rights With Competing Notions of Personhood and Agency in Botswana," in

Harri Enlund and Francis B. Nyamnjoh, eds., *Rights and the Politics of Recognition in Africa* (London: Zed Books, 2004), 33-63, at 57.

[27] Ian S. Markham, *Plurality and Christian Ethics* (Cambridge, Massachusetts: Cambridge University Press, 1994), 189.

[28] Iris Marion Young, *Justice and the Politics of Difference* (New Jersey: Princeton University Press, 1990), 156-163.

[29] Clifford G. Christians, Theodore L. Glasser et al., *Normative Theories of the Media: Journalism in Democratic Societies* (Chicago: University of Illinois Press, 2009), 96.

[30] Robert A. Dahl, *Pluralist Democracy in the United States: Conflict and Consent* (Chicago: Rand McNally, 1967), 24.

[31] Fred Dallmayr, "Democracy and Difference," in Seyla Benhabib, ed., *Democracy and Difference* (New Jersey: Princeton University Press, 1996), 278-294, at 289.

[32] John Courtney Murray, *We Hold These Truths* (Kansas City: Sheed and Ward, 1960), 70-120.

[33] Reinhold Niebuhr, *The Children of the Light and the Children of the Darkness: A Vindication of Democracy and a Critique of Its Traditional Defense* (New York: Charles Scribner's Sons, 1944), xi.

[34] Ibid., 81.

[35] Ibid.

[36] David Hollenbach, S.J., *The Global Face of Public Faith: Politics, Human Rights, and Christian Ethics* (Washington, D.C.: Georgetown University Press, 2003), 240.

[37] Alasdair MacIntyre, *Dependent Rational Animals: Why Human Beings Need the Virtues* (Illinois: Carus Publishing Company, 1999), 131.

[38] The convergence of different spheres of justice is clearly elaborated by Aristotle, *Nicomachean Ethics*, translated by Martin Ostwald (Indianapolis: Bobbs-Merril, 1962), Book V; Michael Walzer, *Spheres of Justice: A Defense of Pluralism and Equality* (New York: Basic Books, 1993); David Hollenbach, S.J., *Justice, Peace, and Human Rights: American Catholic Social Ethics in a Pluralistic World* (New York: Crossroad, 1990).

[39] Michael J. Sandel, *Justice: What's the Right Thing to Do?* (New York: Farrar, Straus, and Giroux, 2009), 244-250.

4. Ethnicity, Citizenship, and Self-Determination

The need to overcome the politics of exclusion, expressed within the dynamics of ethnicity, must be extended to the task of redefining the concepts of ethnicity and citizenship. The importance arises because the debate on citizenship brings forth the challenge of examining the tension between ethnic identity and national identity. Other challenges that come into play include the claim that ethnic diversity raises crucial challenges when certain individuals, groups, and communities are excluded from national projects on the ground of ethnic affiliation. Subsequently any study attempting to comprehend the relationship between ethnicity and citizenship must also examine the determinants of immigration policies, which include the relationship between citizenship and nationhood, and multiculturalism and integration.

In order to address the challenge of reconciling ethnicity, citizenship, and nationalism, we must provide answers to the following questions: Are we likely to witness an end to the recurrent eruption of ethnic-related movements of exclusion, secession, and conflict? Can we preserve ethnic diversity without jeopardizing national unity? Will ethnic tendencies of exclusion and marginalization fade away as people get absorbed into the movements of intermarriage, urbanization, globalization, and democratization? Can ethnic citizenship and national citizenship be reconciled in the process of nation-building? Can we identify other criteria of belonging and citizenship besides blood affiliation and ethnic identity? A balanced response to these questions could facilitate the process of political integration.

Millions of people, because of the forced migration, are stateless because their places of birth were not officially documented.[1] In the course of time the situation has developed into crises of identity and citizenship. The situation has also been aggravated by citizenship policies that render the relationships between ethnic groups problematic. The politics of ethnicity and citizenship are complex and precarious. Even those who have managed to obtain identification their status of citizenship is questioned when they have to renew official documents.[2] A narrow definition of identity and multiple characteristics of ethnicity and citizenship have become a source of exclusion, marginalization, and conflict, and by extension, the condition obstructs efforts geared to promote nation-building. Besides, the introduction of democratic ideals in public institutions has exposed theoretical and practical challenges attached to the relationship between ethnicity and citizenship. The challenge of formulating a common basis for citizenship cannot be ignored insofar as we want to transcend attitudes exclusion, marginalization, and conflict.

The aim of this chapter is to evaluate the impact of ethnicity on the politics of citizenship within the framework of a nation-state.[3] In search for methodologies that can guarantee continuity between ethnicity and nation-state, the discussion unveils six areas of contention that require in-depth analyses, namely, forced migration, management of ethnic diversity, tension between ethnic identity and national identity, relationship between ethnicity, citizenship, and nation-state, evolving concepts of ethnicity and citizenship, and education for responsible citizenship.

Forced Migration and Public Order

The region of Eastern Africa has been severely affected by a wave of forced migration due to the prolonged armed conflicts. The situation has displaced many people, with the consequence of increased insecurity, lawlessness, hunger, and disease. The political situation surrounding these countries, especially Burundi, Rwanda, Sudan, Eritrea, and Somalia, remains volatile and unpredictable. The increased number of internally-displaced people and refugees aggravated the condition of disorder within the realm of socio-political organization, which includes the lack of a clear meaning of citizenship. Such a situation results into the rise of the attitude of exclusion expressed through the dynamics of ethnicity and citizenship.[4]

The condition of widespread insecurity produced an influx of refugees and internally-displaced people. Because of insecurity, the focus shifted from refugee crisis to socio-political crisis. The situation became worse because refugees were confined in camps for many years without being considered for permanent settlement.[5] Most of the aforementioned countries became simultaneously refugee-producing and refugee-receiving countries. Failure to find a permanent solution to the crisis increased socio-political instability, which later on affected the meaning of citizenship, thereby perpetuating the sentiments of exclusion and marginalization. The phenomenon of forced migration and internal displacement created a crisis over the concepts of membership and belonging. As the problem remained unresolved, other problems that emerged include un-belonging and denationalization. The relationship between exclusion from citizenship rights and conflicts is recognized as a potential condition that relates to other political problems. The phenomenon of forced migration has resulted into the loss of the status of citizenship due to the lack of proper documentation of the population.

Inadequacies in the functioning of citizenship have contributed to a widespread uncertainty within the structure of nation-state which, in turn, has become the source of political instability. Similarly, the unresolved citizenship problem of cross-border communities has become a part of the challenge to the nation-state. For instance, in some countries there are separate processes for issuing identity cards, because some members are required to prove that they are not illegal immigrants. Such a situation has ended-up perpetuating the attitudes of discrimination and exclusion. In search for a better future, there is a need to establish a comprehensive understanding of how the dynamics of exclusion function at local, national, and international levels. The dynamics surrounding the loss or acquisition of citizenship could enhance refinement of the existing principles of regulating citizenship.

Resolving the challenges of forced migration, statelessness, and exclusion on the basis of ethnicity is in fact the objective of the analysis. In many ways, the analysis is a tentative exploration because many of these problems have rarely been the object of reflection in the policymaking procedure, governance, and social organization. The following analysis is not shaped into a single system; rather, what is presented in the discussion tries to lay the groundwork for further reflection with the aim of promoting public awareness in the way we approach the dynamics of ethnicity and citizenship. Such openness is required because the issue of forced migration underscores the contradictions that exist between national security and human insecurity, national sovereignty and human rights, and citizenship and immigration.

Management of Ethnic Diversity

The challenge of managing ethnic diversity is gradually intensifying as many nations become culturally and religiously diversified, and, consequently ethnic groups within these nations claim cultural autonomy. There are three reasons attributed to the mismanagement of ethnic diversity. First, the political manipulation of ethnicity has, to a large extent, prevented the emergence of cohesive political societies based on ethnic identities. Second, the framework of nation-state has failed to consolidate diverse ethnic traditions to form cohesive political societies. Third, the ideology of nationalism required citizens to be uniform.[6] Such a situation, unfortunately, produced endless misunderstandings in most countries composed of several ethnic communities. Today, five decades after independence, a number of nation-states are still struggling to overcome the challenge of reversing expectations raised during the time of independence, which made people to think that nationalism would be able to transcend ethnic division. We are also facing a generalized challenge related to the movements of people, commodity, and information that generate a permanent flow of individuals without commitments, rights without duties, and dissemination of information without a sense of discretion. Such a situation presents a challenge because responsible citizenship entails commitment and accountability.

Since ethnic identification is always attached to the communication of cultural differences, cultural traditions become a crucial factor in the management of ethnic diversity. The organization of institutions, to a large extent, influences inter-ethnic interaction by modifying cultural traditions. Management of ethnic diversity correlates to the provisions revolving around the concepts of identity, belonging, rights, and duties. Nevertheless, one of the difficulties encountered by emerging nation-states lies in the challenge of managing ethnic diversity and promoting equal citizenship. The difficulty arises from the fact that ethnic cleavage provides the ground for unhealthy competition. In the context of seeking to build national identities, through ethnic alignments, the situation subverts development, especially when it coincides with economic disparity and political disintegration.

The existence of overlapping traditions and norms testifies that ethnic diversity cannot be a permanent obstacle in the process of building a democratic culture. Such an argument justifies the claim that institutional organization can depoliticize areas of contention. This initiative, however, requires institutions to be structured in such a way that they can encourage people to develop inclusive attitudes. Free interaction and mutual accommodation promote inclusion as a means that can transcend destructive competition and enmity between ethnic groups. The management of ethnic diversity and ethnic-state relations varies from one society to another.

The dream of transcending ethnic prejudice could be realized through the process of cultivating the virtues of tolerance and dialogue. It is possible to create institutional structures that can accommodate cultural diversity by using strategies designed to secure political compromise. Such a project requires us to formulate effective methodologies of managing ethnic diversity instead of upholding methodologies that intend to eliminate cultural differences.[7] An approach of this kind upholds the politics of decentralization that takes seriously the principles of subsidiarity and mutual accommodation as a way of promoting participation, interdependence, and self-determination.

Because of the prevailing ethnic, cultural, and religious diversity, education for citizenship needs to be promoted as a way of preparing people to function responsibly and creatively in multicultural societies. Citizens need knowledge to function effectively within their cultural communities and beyond. In many ways people could be persuaded to maintain attachments to their cultural communities as well as participate responsibly in the shared national culture.[8] Unity without diversity results into repression. In a similar fashion one could argue that diversity without unity leads to the disintegration of the nation-state. The search for a balance between diversity and unity is an ongoing process that cannot be fully attained at once.[9] To achieve such a balance we must acknowledge that cultural particularity is not an extreme position; each culture is expected to find the ground of a deeper unity with other cultures by plunging into the depth of its own cultural resources. The deeper it goes the closer to one another it would get. There can be no meaningful unity of cultures without upholding the selfhood of each culture. Such justification upholds the claim that the unity of a nation-state must be pursued as a complex interplay of differentiated cultural communities brought together for the greater good. It is because of the convergence of particularities and differences that unity of a nation-state become possible.

From Ethnic Identity to National Identity

A number of nations are facing the challenge of how to cope with ethnic, cultural, and religious diversity. The influence of ethnic identity remains strong because social groups require collective identity to claim their rights. Identity, as an evolving process of negotiation, produces a sense of personhood embedded in socio-political interactions. The tension between ethnic identity and national arises when a social group believes to experience exclusion from the political process and wealth distribution.

A pursuit of national identity requires concerted effort sustained by traditions and institutions. In many ways, nevertheless, the idea of forming a national identity remains problematic because of the lack of a common platform of identification. Ethnic identity, which forms the base of national identity, is immutable, while national identity is a process in constant negotiation with its constituent groups. Another challenge that comes into play, where there is polarity between ethnicity and nation-state, is the need to draw a clear distinction between political dynamics and cultural traditions within the process of nation-building. There is incoherence between ethnicity and nation-state when each claim to offer citizenship to all irrespective of cultural difference, but, in reality, each defines citizenship in a way that gives priority to the sectarian interest. It is this incoherence that renders the management of ethnic-state relations problematic.[10]

Critics, from a nationalistic standpoint, argue that ethnic identification must give way to a broader civic identity of nation-state. Justifications given are founded upon the claim that transformation is gradually occurring because of the continuing social change. Others argue that ethnic politics is a temporary phenomenon attached to the desire of self-determination intending to challenge forces of domination. For them, as soon as we establish democratic institutions, ethnocentrism will fade away because movements of ethnicity are forces of political pressure configured to challenge injustice. But, in reality, the influence of ethnic identities on politics, economics, and religion does not show the sign of receding.

Ethnic nationalism is generally characterized as defensive and limited to the collective memory of the ethnic community. Its main focus is to preserve group identity, expressed in terms of blood relationship and place of birth to guarantee self-determination. Such a tendency is established through isolation from other ethnic groups. Critics argue that because of the growing interaction between social groups, institutionalization of ethnicity is gradually becoming irrelevant. Others claim that the urge of preserving cultural identities, normally, tends to cling to the collective memory that generates cultural anxiety. Such an experience suggests that ethno-cultural nationalism must be encouraged to acquire an attitude of inclusion that upholds the ethical principle of pluralism expressed in terms of tolerance, inclusion, and multiculturalism.

In a number of societies people identify themselves in terms of ethnic affiliation disregarding the relevance of nation-state. In my opinion there is nothing wrong with the structure of nation-state. Justification for nation-state lies in its ability to unify local communities in the sense that it can secure minimum conditions to form a cohesive political society. The process of constructing an inclusive structure of nation-state cannot be reversed. It is unrealistic, at this time in history, to think of returning to the ethnic fiefdoms of the past. The framework of nation-state generates a functional political unit as well as trans-cultural engagement that can secure common identity, cohesion, and security.

For self-identification, identity cards and passports make a difference. They determine whether one is a naturalized citizen or a citizen by birth, with the consequences each category generates. Symbols of identification can also generate mutual suspicion as it has been the case in Côte d'Ivoire, where the ideology of *Ivoirité* determines whether one is authentically Ivorian or not.[11] Extending the concept of ethnic identity to citizenship has caused political unrest, because the criterion of *Ivoirité* created rivalry between those who claim to be originally from Côte d'Ivoire against those who are naturalized, but considered as second class immigrants originating from the neighboring countries.[12] In the context of Côte d'Ivoire, the place of birth generates implications that determine the modalities of allocating rights and duties. Clearly, the situation reveals a challenge of bridging local custom and state law in the process of molding national identity.[13] Such a phenomenon occurred in the Eastern part of the Democratic Republic of Congo by pointing out the Banyamulenge people as unwanted immigrants, thereby generating an endless hostility between the Democratic Republic of Congo and Rwanda. Another similar example is found among the Nubians and the Somalis living between Sudan, Kenya, and Somalia.[14] All these people are widely regarded as stateless and unwanted by any country.

The tension surrounding citizenship derives from the polarity between ethnic identity and national identity. Such a situation compels us to ask ourselves the following question: Does the concept of national identity necessarily derive from cultural identity? Any attempt intending to bridge political nationalism and cultural nationalism could generate tension between ethnicity and nationalism. Should we define people's identity by following the criterion of cultural identity or national identity? The example of Côte d'Ivoire pointed out earlier is a case in point here. Can naturalized immigrants be fully accorded rights without any form of marginalization? Differently stated, can those who are citizens through the process of naturalization acquire the same status as those who are citizens by birth? The policymakers have failed to produce a satisfactory answer to the question.

For a society to flourish there must be local communities willing to form persons whose identity is bound-up in relationships that transcend attitudes of isolation and exclusion. The politics of building national identity must ensure that individuals and local communities do not distance themselves from inherited traditions because such an extreme could damage the foundations of cultural consciousness.[15] Instead, local communities should aim at forming an individual whose life is interwoven with a larger public whole. Without inter-personal and inter-communal relationships, the isolated individual and community cannot sustain themselves but collapse in the self-reference, and given these circumstances, society ends up paying the price. A genuine political society is composed of individuals and groups who participate in sharing common identity as well as celebrate their distinctiveness. Such a society is not quickly formed; rather, it gains its form and character in the course of time.

The preceding discussion has already unveiled challenges attached to the definition of national identity. We argued that the claims of ethnic-state relations are manageable insofar as each party recognizes the role of the other. The model of identity politics considers identity as a political variable because it is essential in building the sense of belonging and commitment. The way in which people perceive themselves is likely to have a significant impact on how they relate to others and how they are motivated to participate in nation-building.

Ethnicity, Citizenship, and Immigration

Ethnicity is a force that affects institutions, citizenship, and nation-state. It plays a constitutive role in the process of molding two forms of citizenship: ethnic citizenship and national citizenship. The difference between ethnic citizenship and national citizenship lies in the sovereign authority and bureaucratic structures that uphold the legitimacy of the nation-state, as opposed to the symbols of identity, customs, and non-bureaucratic structures that uphold ethnic citizenship.[16] The variable of identity plays a determinant role in both forms of citizenship by demarcating the

74

boundaries of belonging. In a post-colonial nation-state, national citizenship is legally enforced by claims of sovereignty within a given territory and bureaucratic symbols of identification. Ethnic identity, which correlates to the concept of belonging, rests upon socio-cultural relations. Such a perspective is opposed to the legal status that forms the base for national identity. That is to say the concept of citizenship is founded upon legal status, while identity is a relational concept suggesting a dialogical recognition between ethnicity and nation-state.

Citizenship could be defined as a "status bestowed on those who are full members of a political community. All who possess the status are equal with respect to the rights and duties with which the status is endowed."[17] It is a legal framework of defining those who are, and those who are not, members of a given society. The status of citizenship, argues Stephen N. Ndegwa, allows a person to belong to a particular community, while enjoying certain rights and being demanded to perform certain duties in return.[18] The provision of citizenship is closely related to the challenge of resolving the problems of belonging and identification. The meaning and content of citizenship is highly contested because it cannot be understood without making reference to ethnicity, which is a sub-national entity in which national citizenship derive. The definition of citizenship, from the standpoint of nationalism, has traditionally been identified with state sovereignty. But challenges emerge when we want to concretize it, because it must make reference to specific identities, persons, cultures, and communities.

The meaning of citizenship remains ambiguous, and in many ways, in the process of defining it, we have to follow the criterion of ethnic identity, which is limited to the place of birth, blood relationship, or state sovereignty. It is evident that the tension between ethnic identity and national identity renders the concept of citizenship difficult to define. In search for a balanced solution one could argue that individuals hold multiple and changing identities, roles, and status depending on the situation in which they find themselves. People, in many ways, experience a convergence of demands arising from two categories of citizenship, namely, ethnic citizenship and national citizenship.[19] For ethnic citizenship, identity is centered on the memory, lineage, and community, and in this case a person involved cannot claim rights that would jeopardize interests of the community he belongs.[20] Individuals are not morally autonomous because rights are accorded to them by community. Rights are secured through the process of participation, which defines, establishes, and sustains the community.[21]

The concept of "citizenship" becomes problematic when the issues of state sovereignty and cultural authenticity emerge. The challenge of forced migration draws attention to the issue of identity. For instance, the ideology of *Ivoirité* refers to the attitude of distinguishing "true Ivorians" from the rest, which includes marginalized immigrants. This ideology, as we have seen, has triggered a political crisis that rendered ethnic citizenship and national citizenship incompatible. The xenophobic attacks on foreigners witnessed in South Africa, 2008, are also based on similar factors.

As people participate in the nation-building, individuals situate as well as limit their expectations within the framework of the ethnic community. In this attachment, for a number of people, nation-state is a means through which to fulfill interests of the ethnic community. Their sphere of influence is limited to the ethnic community, and, as such, the involvement in the public sphere is only a means to achieve sectarian interests. Making reference to such an attitude one could conclude that ethnic citizenship is limited to the local customs, place of birth, and blood relationship, while national citizenship is civic, legal, and trans-ethnic. In the case of national citizenship, the transfer of allegiance is secured by acquiring a sense of belonging to a larger political community.

Citizenship, from the viewpoint of ethnicity, is justified by following the criteria of identity and belonging to an ethnic community. Ethnic citizenship evokes cultural difference for the benefit of the ethnic community. The authority of ethnic citizenship is strongly vested in blood relationship, while the authority of national citizenship is vested in legal procedures. The understanding of citizenship in terms of nationalism is challenged by recognition of local communities as avenues that specify the content of citizenship. For Mahmood Mamdani, "ethnic community is the source of a different category of rights. These rights are not accessed individually but by virtue of group membership, the group being the ethnic community."[22] With such understanding, one could conclude that ethnic community is a framework of belonging and accountability.

From a standpoint of nationalism, "citizenship encompasses legal status, participation, rights, duties, and belonging, traditionally encored in a particular territory and political community."[23] The concept of citizenship evokes notions of national identity, state sovereignty, equal participation, and security; but, on the other hand, it is challenged by the concepts of particularity and diversity. The character of these attributes reveals that the meaning of citizenship navigates between exclusion and inclusion.[24] Does the meaning of citizenship derive from the dynamics of ethno-cultural identity or legally-established procedure? Such a question suggests that ethnic citizenship and national citizenship are interrelated.

Political leaders are still living under conditions in which the easiest way to hold on power is to mobilize one's community for support, and then do whatever is necessary to ensure that other communities are antagonized. Such a situation shows that national identity, in search for cohesion, must transcend inter-ethnic antagonism by acquiring characteristics that can redefine the meaning of citizenship. These characteristics, in search for mutual accommodation, include tolerance, dialogue, and the common good. These values challenge the politics of exclusion, discrimination, and favoritism. The ideal situation would be that aspirants campaigning for leadership must be encouraged to concentrate on issues of development rather than appealing for votes using the criterion of ethnic affiliation. People can relate beyond ethnic affiliation by focusing on common fears, needs, and expectations, which include whether one has a job, education, security, and healthcare.

At this stage of the discussion I propose to bridge the concepts of migration, naturalization, and citizenship. The form of citizenship accorded by culture puts an accent on ethnic identity in terms of language, tradition, and solidarity, while national citizenship follows more the criteria of equal rights, state sovereignty, and legal requirements than cultural identity which tend to put an emphasis on the place of birth. National citizenship is political, territorial, legal, and civic. Ethno-cultural conception of citizenship is one way of determining membership in the political community. Focusing on migration and naturalization, one could argue that the process of granting citizenship is more influenced by the criteria of economic well-being, state security, political order, state sovereignty, and legal procedure than cultural identity which tends to put an emphasis on the place of birth and cultural identity. Critics argue that cultural attachments are partially sacrificed when procedures of national citizenship are followed. By following these arguments, one could conclude that whereas ethnicity emphasizes differences between groups, nationalism concentrates on participatory rights.

Again, experience shows that people operate with dual citizenship: one for ethnic community and another for the nation-state. These two forms of citizenship operate at different levels of social organization and interaction, and they differ in form and content. At the level of ethnic citizenship, the focus is centered on preserving community identity. In this case people are only accountable to the ethnic community. Such an experience shows that there is a lack of continuity from ethnic citizenship to national citizenship. That is why there is a lack of commitment at the national level, especially in the areas of leadership and governance, which results into practices of looting the state, corruption, and other forms of irresponsibility.

Granting the status of citizenship by following the criteria of the place of birth and ethnic identity could perpetuate sentiments of exclusion and marginalization. How can we establish legitimate ways of identifying people if we take into account the undocumented immigrants in this era of global interaction? Can any political organization ignore the concepts ethnic identity and place of birth in identifying people? The current struggle for nation-states includes the challenge of answering these questions.

We can draw seven conclusions from the preceding discussion. First, the status of citizenship and the common good refer to ethnic identities, because these realities cannot be understood besides cultural identities and political emotions. These two variables are intrinsically attached to the formation of attitude and character, and, as such, they are the basis for membership and collective identity. Second, exclusion is a common denominator for ethnicity and citizenship. Third, the condition of political disintegration is caused by the lack of ability to create as well as maintain interdependence and continuity between ethnicity, citizenship, and nation-state. Fourth, the challenges raised in the discussion suggest that there is a need to renegotiate the exclusionary bases of citizenship that fuel misunderstanding over belonging and representation. This means we have to re-conceptualize citizenship in ways that can create space for those who suffer exclusion. Such a project must be governed by a concept of citizenship unbounded by the politics of exclusion.[25] Fifth, there is a need to expand the horizon of ethnicity as well as challenge the thinking that a nation-state is the only entity that can confer the status of citizenship. Sixth, a polarized relationship between ethnicity and nation-state pose a threat to the meaning of citizenship. Seventh, the effort of building a national culture must focus on dynamic and open-ended approaches toward the concepts of identity, ethnicity, and citizenship.

Evolving Concepts of Ethnicity and Citizenship
The meaning and content of ethnicity and citizenship are constantly changing depending on the prevailing political conditions. Efforts to identify legitimate citizenship remain at large unsuccessful. The change of meaning for a particular concept is caused by the changing conditions of life, empirically and metaphysically, to which the concept is applied.[26] Such a situation results from the increase of diversity in terms of culture and religion.

Similarly the increasing mobility of people raises new issues for ethnicity and citizenship. The question that arises is that can we constitute a meaning of citizenship without considering the import of cultural identity? The concepts of ethnicity and citizenship could be refashioned by transcending the rigid understanding of identity, belonging, and place of birth. In order to guarantee equal participation, the meaning of citizenship should not be limited to ethnic identity and place of birth; rather, it should be presented as a political community without any claim to common cultural identity. This argument is significant because it takes seriously the possibility of migration and acknowledgement of common citizenship. The traditional meaning of ethnicity and citizenship that have been limited to cultural identity and place of birth are no longer adequate in organizing modern societies. Reconciling the individual and the community is the key to the problem of citizenship characterized by movements of migration, urbanization, and globalization. Integration of people of diverse cultures and beliefs require broadening of the meaning of participation. Such a possibility could be realized insofar as the concept of citizenship is influenced by concepts of diversity and inclusion.

The ambiguities of ethnicity and citizenship emerge from the fact of having two unequal categories of citizenship: active citizenship and passive citizenship. Active citizenship is accorded to those who are permitted to exercise political power, while passive citizenship is accorded to those who are not permitted to exercise political power.[27] Such a situation, politically, endorses unequal citizenship and exclusion. This challenge remains unresolved when we refer to the concept of naturalization. My observation is that passive citizens, in many ways, are marginalized citizens, and it is absurd to talk about equal citizenship where there is structural injustice. Boldly stated, passive citizenship is limited due to the lack of equal participation. The rights of the passive citizens are significantly reduced because of the lack of the place of birth and cultural identity in the society they are naturalized. Political decisions are made by active citizens, whereas passive citizens remain excluded from the political process.

Many societies, today, are multicultural. Such a situation attests that there is an existence of segmented social groups that can establish effective political cohesion within the society. By extension, the same argument is used to propagate cultural, economic, and political claims on the basis of group identity. Sometimes class becomes congruent with ethnicity, especially where there is a bipolar situation in which one ethnic group is predominant and another ethnic group marginalized. Where class issues have become politicized, the ethnic affiliation becomes salient. Ethnicity becomes important because it can link interest with group affiliation.[28] In this case ethnicity provides a tangible identification when other social roles become impersonal. On the other hand, ethnicity has become an avenue for promoting rights-claims when other mechanisms of promoting social justice have failed. The possibility of multiple meanings render ethnicity ambiguous for it becomes constructive or destructive depending on how we appeal to it. That is to say ethnicity can be congruent to sectarianism, exclusion, and discrimination, as opposed to identity, loyalty, and solidarity.

In trying to account for the upsurge of ethnicity, one can argue that ethnicity, as an emergent expression of identities, suppressed by the forces of nationalism, has now been reawakened as a new mode of seeking political justice that can challenge the state. In this case ethnicity becomes a means of demanding group rights. Ineffectiveness of state makes the paradigm of ethnicity important. Another way of understanding ethnicity involves manipulating it for private interest and privilege. We can therefore conclude that concepts of ethnicity and citizenship do not have static meaning. As we have pointed out earlier it all depends on the prevailing circumstances of life. Since ethnicity and citizenship are evolving concepts, then, nationalism, by extension, becomes also an evolving concept because its meaning is founded upon the content of ethnicity and citizenship.

How does the change of meaning and content of ethnicity and citizenship occur? The fact is that people from different cultural systems have different conceptions of the human person and the good life. This correlation validates the claim that cultural differences justify contextualization of moral knowledge. Such perspectives mold diverse understandings of ethnicity and citizenship. I wish, however, to argue that traditions themselves are subject to change insofar as the conditions of life change. Static cultural traditions and moral norms do not exist. The encounter between value systems provides the stage where different understandings converge. Such a convergence is justified by human dignity and the common good that leads to the overlapping consensus of the concepts of ethnicity and citizenship.

A moral agent is situated at the crossroads of different dimensions of historical consciousness. To dismiss any dimension is to misunderstand the complexity of morality. The point of contention is that a moral action is complex in the sense that it always contains different variables that ought to be considered in moral discernment. It is not simply the significance of certain elements that matters, but the significance of how all the elements that constitute the whole interact to produce meaning. The concern is not simply to realize certain elements and dimensions of the moral agent taken in isolation; rather, it is the question of focusing on the entire complex web of multiple dimensions of human experience. Interpreting human action entails evaluating a human person as a whole. Nothing that influences the process of human consciousness should be left out. Diverse dimensions of human experience fashion the perception, attitude, and character of the moral agent. Based on this observation I argue that the effort of promoting citizenship rights is an enterprise that requires consideration of different experiences arising from different dimensions of human experience and social institutions.

The dynamics of change depend on the formation of the moral agent in relation to the context of life and cultural traditions. The interdependence of these dimensions fashions the value system that anchors the dynamics of ethnicity and citizenship. This approach takes into account three key points: that there is a need to theorize out of experience rather than to allow theory to limit experience; that it is wrong to start with abstract norms and then seek to justify their applicability in particular cultures and contexts; and that moral traditions emerge from specific contexts of life, value systems, and worldviews.[29] While accepting that cultural diversity could strengthen rights discourse it is also appropriate to admit that cultural traditions are limited, and as such they need regular evaluation, self-criticism, and transformation. The weaknesses of cultural relativism include rigidity, self-centeredness, and isolationism. Radical relativism upholds that moral traditions are unchangeable. But cultural traditions and moral norms are always subject to change. With this in mind, one could argue that ethnicity and citizenship, as social constructs, should not be approached as ends-in-themselves; instead, they should be approached as realities which are open to change. Following these arguments one could conclude that the meaning of ethnicity and citizenship are not static; rather, they are constantly changing insofar as they are subjected to contestation from within and without.

Moral norms are embedded in a complex web of diverse experiences arising from social relationships. Ethical norms are situated within the historical-cultural realities in which moral agents are nurtured. Efforts geared to promote citizenship rights must be more than a mere application of a set of laws. They have to take into account diverse experiences of life in terms of value systems and cultural traditions. In order to understand the contemporary challenge of promoting inclusion and equal citizenship one must go beyond a mere rediscovery of traditional belief systems, cultural traditions, and political ideologies. One must venture to take seriously the innovation of moral norms. Such an enterprise requires creative thinking and localized initiative. Attempts to contextualize ethnicity and citizenship debate should not be seen as ill-founded efforts intended to destroy what has been achieved; rather, we should see these efforts as a manifestation of moral maturity that intend to promote inclusion from the viewpoint of social relationships. Moral norms are historical because cultural configurations of symbols and circumstances are in constant change; and as such moral norms have meaning in relation to the changing field of action.[30] The trajectory of a moving field of values must be traced vis-à-vis the changing conditions of life. This is precisely how to comprehend the changing meanings of ethnicity and citizenship. And, as such, the meanings of ethnicity and citizenship must be continuously re-analyzed, re-evaluated, and re-created.

Education for Responsible Citizenship

Ethnicity is a crucial variable in the process of molding a nation-state. The process occurs when the dynamics of ethnicity involves subjective identification and inter-subjective communication. A normative system forms a matrix of shared norms and communicative resources that constitute a cultural basis for social interaction. At the grassroots level, the narratives of formation function when ethnic identities influence attitudes of individuals in the inter-subjective encounters. At the national level, institutions strive to translate ethnic identities into coalitions that can influence social interaction.

Education for citizenship is founded upon the cultivation of civic virtues and civic engagement.[31] It provides a framework that allows us to negotiate the demands of living in multicultural societies and how to collaborate with those whose traditions we may not share. This kind of education promotes a sense of public reasonableness by dealing with collective identity, political membership, and rights underlying socio-political entitlements. Education for citizenship enables citizens to take responsibility for their own lives and communities they belong. This kind of formation goes beyond conceptual knowledge and uniformity, because it focuses on promoting civic engagement through tolerance, dialogue, and involvement. The concept of citizenship, in this case, brings with it the sense of rights and duties. It refers not only to rights and duties laid down in the law, but also to the power of virtues. It is the process of helping people to learn how to become engaged, informed, and responsible. Justification for citizenship education derives from the ideals of democracy that require citizens to participate in the political process. Citizens who take responsibility for the communities they belong contribute to the process of nation-building.

The challenges of the modern world require us to seek shared understanding with which to make decisions founded upon mutual understanding. Such a platform emerges insofar as there is a harmonized moral formation. Citizenship education, remarks Will Kymlicka, "is not just the matter of learning the basic facts about the institutions and procedures of political life; rather, it also involves acquiring a range of dispositions, virtues, and loyalties that are bound up with the practice of democracy."[32] The argument of Kymlicka confirms that it is unrealistic to expect formal education, on its own, to fully promote the virtues required for responsible citizenship. The role of the family, neighborhood, religion, and association is indispensable. The challenge of promoting shared civic identity requires a concerted effort designed to promote shared civic virtues at all levels of social interaction. The institutional mechanisms of balancing interests are not enough. The awareness of moral responsibility requires also the cultivation of virtues in all dimensions of human experience. Formation for citizenship is indispensable, because it is a gateway to the formation of just society. The process occurs by producing people who relate amicably to each other. Such a process helps people who are willing to participate in the life of the nation-building. We cannot establish democratic institutions without having citizens who know their rights and duties. Such a process of formation promotes aptitudes of critical thinking, analysis, reflection, and action. Formation to acquire virtues of disposition toward justice, tolerance, and dialogue require investment in terms of moral instruction and civic engagement.

Education for responsible citizenship is designed to help people develop strong attachment to their cultural communities and nations. Such initiative is paramount because disordered cultural attachments obstruct the process of forming a nation with clearly defined objectives. Cultural, national, and international identifications are interrelated, and as such people must be encouraged to develop a delicate balance of cultural, national, and international identifications. A nation that does not include all cultural groups into the national culture runs the risk of creating alienation that could encourage social groups to focus on secession rather than overarching objectives of the society.

It is imperative to note that in every social issue people hold diverse and incompatible viewpoints. We have entered an era in which the history of humankind is shaped by the value of inclusion as a means of moving away from exclusion to the recognition of pluralism and interdependence. Since the last century people have arrived at a revolutionary understanding of public life. The euphoria of uniformity and imposition of one's conviction on others are not plausible in the modern world. The desire to exercise freedom of choice, participation, and respect of diversity has become paramount in public life.

Tolerance, as a virtue of mutual accommodation, could be described as a simple recognition of the fact that there are different ways of seeing things. Such occurrence is reinforced through the claim that there are different value systems shaped by incompatible understandings of the good life. This means pluralism has become a condition that guarantees numerous social groups to live together peacefully. Engaged tolerance is not simply otherness and difference; rather, it refers to the fact that individuals and groups bring to the public sphere diverse perspectives for mutual enrichment. Pluralism entails holding one's own identities while at the same time cooperate with others to enhance common good. It is about building relationships that can enhance the virtue of mutual accommodation. The assumption put forward here is that all religions and cultures are legitimate and as such they ought to be respected. Such an argument presupposes diversity and interdependence. Conflicts over cultural differences must not be viewed as conflicts between contenting truths but as conflict of interests that could be resolved through dialogue and mutual respect. The virtue of tolerance encourages appreciation of diversity as well as exercise of respect toward the opinion of others. Tolerance is not just remaining indifferent in the face of injustice; rather, it is about showing respect toward others.[33] It is the ability to exercise fairness toward those whose opinion, religion, and culture differ from one's own. Mutual accommodation facilitates communication and peaceful coexistence between individuals and groups with divergent and incompatible traditions as a process of promoting mutual understanding.

Initiatives attempting to draw wisdom from the African traditional education systems to challenge attitudes of exclusion must acknowledge that there are a number of shortcomings that must be challenged.[34] Such weaknesses include the fact that the traditional forms of education did not focus so much on social change, because they over-emphasized conformity by demanding strict obedience to the elders' authority, which gave no room for imagination, creativity, and criticism. What mattered most was to follow inherited traditions. A genuine search for a balanced formation for citizenship should therefore focus on the ethics of inclusion as a means of promoting transformation of social structures and social relationships.

Conclusion

The objective of the discussion has been to solicit new meanings of ethnicity and citizenship consistent with the principles of participation, inclusion, and equality. Ethnic discrimination accounts as one of the driving forces that has contributed and continues to undermine political advancement. Despite the problems encountered, apparently, many countries continue to pursue the objective of building a common national identity. The prevailing situation compels us to find out what we have learned from the experience of failed states and how we should proceed in search for a better future. We are all aware of the numerous difficulties involved in expressing the perspectives of multiple traditions in dealing with complex socio-political matters. The challenges raised by current socio-political situation demand that we seek shared understandings with which to make constructive decisions.

The challenge of reconciling the dynamics of ethnicity, citizenship, and nationalism does not pertain to the relic of the past; rather, it is a required art for organizing modern societies. Similarly the prevailing challenge of forced migration raises serious questions toward the concept of citizenship, with the main concern revolving around the demands of rights and duties. Issues related to the exclusion of the undocumented immigrants and minorities cannot be ignored in the process of building a democratic culture, because the problems related to ethnicity and citizenship are necessarily related to the rights of immigrants and minorities.

The challenge of exclusion on the basis of ethnic affiliation is not limited to Africa; rather, it exists everywhere. The only difference is that it is expressed in different forms: tribalism in Africa, caste system in Asia, and racism in Europe and North America. In search for an appropriate response to the issues raised in the discussion we have to undertake the following assignments: first, use the import of the discussion as a basis for inter-disciplinary dialogue; second, encourage everybody to reflect critically on how the principle of democratic governance can engage everybody in the process of nation-building; and third, use suggestions provided to promote common citizenship. Such an engagement is the key for the future of the continent of Africa in terms of promoting public order, social justice, and citizenship rights.

Notes

---

[1] A well-researched work on the challenge of statelessness is presented by Browen Manby, *Struggles for Citizenship in Africa* (London: Zed Books Ltd, 2009), 12-52.

[2] RAS Editor, "The Politics of Citizenship in Africa: Debate Overview," *http://africanarguments.org/2010/09/who-belongs-the-politics-of-citizenship-in-africa-debate-overview* (Accessed on October, 25, 2010).

[3] I do not wish to present a comprehensive historical evolution of ethnicity and citizenship debates, apology, or a list of specific citizenship rights from the perspective of theology, philosophy, anthropology, or political science. Such studies have been already undertaken, extensively, in the last decade. My intention is to evaluate the impact of these variables within the context of contemporary Africa without being rendered captive to theoretical disputes. Such engagement will be able to address the prevailing challenges encountered by returning refugees, especially statelessness, exclusion, and marginalization.

[4] Stephanie J. Nawyn, "Faith, Ethnicity, and Culture in Refugee Resettlement," *American Behavioral Scientist*, 49, 11 (July, 2006): 1510; Peter Kanyandago, "Who is My Neighbor? A Christian Response to Refugees and the Displaced in Africa," in J. N. K. Mugambi and Anne Nasimiyu-Wasike, eds., *Moral and Ethical Issues in African Christianity* (Nairobi: Initiatives Publishers, 1992), 173.

[5] A good example is Kakuma Refugee Camp located in Turkana District, in the North-Eastern region of Kenya. This camp has served refugees who fled civil wars, for many years, from the neighboring countries, mainly, Sudan, Somalia, Uganda, Rwanda, Burundi, Eritrea, Ethiopia, and the Democratic Republic of Congo. For further reading, see Cassandra R. Veney, *Forced Migration in Eastern Africa: Democratization, Structural Adjustment, and Refugees* (Pennsylvania: Palgrave MacMillan, 2006); Ebenezer Q. Blavo, The Problems of Refugees in Africa:

Boundaries and Borders (London: Ashgate, 1990); David Hollenbach, S.J., ed., *Driven from Home: Protecting the Rights of Forced Migrants* (Washington, D.C.: Georgetown University Press, 2010); Sewe K'Ahenda, ed., *A Theological Response to the Tragedy of Refugees and Internally Displaced Persons in Africa* (Nairobi: CUEA Publications, 2007).

[6] John Hutchinson and Anthony D. Smith, eds., *Ethnicity* (Oxford: Oxford University Press, 1996), Introduction.

[7] Crawford Young, ed., *Ethnic Diversity and Public Policy: An Overview* (Geneva: Macmillan, 1998), 1-30.

[8] James A. Banks, "Diversity, Group Identity, and Citizenship Education in a Global Age," *Educational Researcher*, 37, 3 (April, 2008): 129-139, at 129.

[9] Ibid., "Educating Global Citizens in a Diverse World," *http://www.newhorizons.org/strategies/multicultural/banks2.htm* (Accessed on September 8, 2010).

[10] David Brown, "Ethnicity, Nationalism, and Democracy," in John Hutchinson and Anthony D. Smith, eds., *Ethnicity* (New York: Oxford University Press, 1996), 305-311, at 307.

[11] Wikipedia: The Free Encyclopedia, "Ivoirité," *http://en.wikipedia.org/wiki/ivoiritec3a9* (Accessed on October 10, 2010). The term "Ivoirité" was initially referred to as a common cultural identity of all people living in Côte d'Ivoire. But xenophobic ideas, fanned by the politics of exclusion, changed it to mean the population from the South and East of the country, thereby excluding those from the North, who are considered to be foreigners coming from the neighboring countries.

[12] Siendou A. Konate, "The Politics of Identity and Violence in Côte d'Ivoire," *West Africa Review*, 5 (February, 2004): 1-15.

[13] For further elaboration on the challenge of linking ethnicity and nationalism, see Adrian Hastings, *The Construction of Nationhood: Ethnicity, Religion, and Nationalism* (Cambridge: Cambridge University Press, 1997), 1-45.

[14] See, for example, the claim made by Adam Hussein Adam, "Kenyan Nubians: Standing Up to Statelessness," *Forced Migration Review*, 32 (April, 2009): 19.

[15] Robert Bellah et al., *Habits of the Heart: Individualism and Commitment in American Life* (San Francisco: Harper & Row, 1985), 153.

[16] National citizenship derives from an idealized conception of the nation-state, which is administratively uniform and centralized, in which citizenship is understood as a legal status. In this understanding, the nation-state is the only locus of political community endowed with absolute authority, and as such the meaning of citizenship is basically confined to it. Proponents of nation-state claim that everyone is supposed to belong to a nation-state. All identities and authorities are fused into nation-states. For critics, these claims arise from unsound logic and uncritical examination of facts, and by implication, new meanings of ethnicity, citizenship, and nation-state must be sought. New conceptions of citizenship within nation-states could provide innovative avenues for promoting participatory democracy.

[17] William Idowu, "Ethnicity, Ethnicism, and Citizenship: A Philosophical Reflection on the African Experience," *Journal of Social Sciences*, 8, 1 (January, 2004): 45-58, at 49.

[18] Stephen N. Ndegwa, "Citizenship and Ethnicity: An Examination of Two Transition Moments in Kenyan Politics," *The American Political Science Review*, 91, 3 (September, 1997): 599-616, at 1; Malcom Walters, "Citizenship and the Constitution of Structures of Social Inequality," *International Journal of Comparative Sociology*, 30 (December, 1989): 159-180, at 160.

[19] Ibid., 603.

[20] On the relationship between identity, culture, and community, see Laurenti Magesa, *African Religion in the Dialogue Debate: From Intolerance to Coexistence* (Zweigniederlssung, Zurich: Lit Verlag, 2010), 19-26; David Miller, "Community and Identity," in Shlomo Avineri and Aviner de-Shalit, eds., *Communitarianism and Individualism* (Oxford: Oxford University Press, 1992), 87-92.

[21] Ibid.

[22] Mahmood Mamdani, *When Victims Become Killers: Colonialism, Nativity, and the Genocide* (New Jersey: Princeton University Press, 2001), 29.

[23] Irene Bloemraad, Anna Korteweg, and Gorkce Yurdakul, "Citizenship and Immigration: Multiculturalism, Assimilation, and Challenges to the Nation-State," *Annual Review of Sociology*, 34 (August, 2008): 153-179, at 153.

[24] Ibid., 154.

[25] A comprehensive justification for the need of flexible citizenship is carefully elaborated by Francis B. Nyamnjoh, "From Bounded to Flexible Citizenship: Lessons from Africa," *Citizenship Studies*, 11, 1 (February, 2007): 73-82.

[26] T. K. Oommen, *Citizenship, Nationality, and Ethnicity: Reconciling Competing Identities* (Oxford: Blackwell Publishers Ltd, 1997), 6.

[27] In some countries if your parents were not born in your present country you cannot become a president. This is also a common regulation in the constitutions of African countries.

[28] Daniel Bell, "Ethnicity and Social Change," in John Hutchinson and Anthony D. Smith, eds., *Ethnicity* (Oxford: Oxford University Press, 1996), 138-146, at 144.

[29] See, for example, Jürgen Habermas, *Moral Consciousness and Communicative Action* (Cambridge, Massachusetts: The MIT Press, 1991), 21-188.

[30] Tod Swanson, "The Persuasive Voice of Oscar Romero," *Journal of Religious Ethics*, 29, 3 (Spring, 2001): 127-144, at 143.

[31] Michael Walzer, "Citizenship," in T. Ball and J. Farra, eds., *Political Innovation and Conceptual Change* (Cambridge: Cambridge University Press, 1989), 211-220.

[32] Will Kymlicka, "Education for Citizenship," in J. Mark Halstead, ed., *Education in Morality* (London: Routledge, 1999), 79-102, at 79.

[33] William Ury, *Getting to Peace* (New York: The Penguin Group, 1999), 127.

[34] See, for example, the analysis of the Acholi culture presented by Jakayo P. Ocitti, *African Indigenous Education as Practiced by*

the Acholi of Uganda (Nairobi: East Africa Literature Bureau, 1973), 45-52.

5. Religion, Politics, and Civil Society

thnicity and religion are two crucial variables that affect the dynamics of leadership, governance, wealth distribution, and political integration. These variables act as a foundational base upon which formation of identity, solidarity, and security occurs. They can overlap, partially or completely, in the process of molding the worldview of the community. If ethnic identities and religious beliefs influence political process, then religion is a variable that cannot be taken for granted in the process of political integration. Along with ethnicity, religion has long been established as a social cleavage generating political competition within the society. Individuals and groups alike mobilize people politically using religious influence as a driving force. Such a dimension produces a powerful political position for individuals and communities. Religious activities are a part of political process, because they play a constitutive role in the process of molding attitude and character.

From the beginning of the exploration, especially in chapter one, I argued that African churches are also caught-up in the web of ethno-political competition. The problem arises from the fact that religious leaders have not yet established clear methodologies of political engagement. With the aim of linking religious virtues to civic virtues, the study evaluates the role and the limitation of religion in the process of political integration. Such a perspective is worthy of consideration because we have to comprehend the appeal to the power of religion in the process of reconstructing social relationships, and its implication in the rise of ethno-religious intolerance affecting shared responsibility to promote socio-political cohesion. Such a connection could challenge the tendency of limiting religious experience to the private sphere as well as unveil reasons that perpetuate sectarianism. Such a study will enlighten the effort of comprehending the influence of religion in the process of political integration.

For many years, movements of enlightenment and secularization have attempted to overshadow the role of religion in the public sphere. The movement of post-modernism has, however, argued that claims made by these movements were unrealistic. In recent years, a number of scholars from various disciplines have argued that the role of religion in the public sphere is indispensable.[1] Similarly, social actors such as human rights activists have confirmed that religion plays a key role in the formation of responsible citizens, and as such it is unrealistic to exclude religion from the public sphere. For them, normally, when religion is excluded from the public life it comes into play through the backdoor. With this kind of challenge at hand it is appropriate to encourage an open involvement in order to minimize the destruction that could be caused when religion is confined to the private sphere.

Religion, whether in the form of religious institutions or religious movements, is a crucial factor that cannot be ignored. Nevertheless, because of the attitude of intolerance, the role of religion in public life raises serious questions. Such questions include: Should religious organizations be tolerated in the political realm, relegated to the private sphere, or suppressed altogether? How does religion collaborate with other agents of civil society in addressing social issues? Does one run the risk of creating an intolerant political sphere simply by allowing religious organizations to play an active role in public life? Can religion promote tolerance, social justice, human rights, and the common good? For a number of people, as these questions suggest, it is difficult to overcome the thinking that religions must separate themselves from political life. Such an attitude derives from the fact that a number of people perceive religion as a conversation-stopper.[2] It is, therefore, appropriate to unveil the causes of the situation as well as propose methodologies that can bring together activities of religion and civil society in the process of addressing socio-political issues.

The way religions engage in the process of political transformation, through public discourse, remains ambiguous. The role of religions in the public life as well as the relationship between religion and civil society remains problematic because of the lack of clear methodologies of civic engagement and institutional collaboration. Many religions are unable to act decisively even when the situation requires immediate response from religious institutions. In the situation of Uganda, Ethiopia, and Kenya, for example, Christian churches tend to present unclear positions in the public, even when the politically motivated forms of violence are killing innocent people. Similarly, whenever there are initiatives from church-related institutions a division between churches and other agents of civil society tend to emerge because of the lack of institutional collaboration and partisan politics among the leaders. Apparently, most of the existing organizations designed to facilitate institutional collaboration are narrow-minded and sectarian. Such a situation calls for a critical examination of the situation as well as seek shared understanding with which to take constructive action.

The objective of this chapter, from the perspective of the local churches within the context of Eastern Africa countries, is to identify ways in which the rediscovered models of small Christian communities and pastoral letters could be used to strengthen the idea of civil society. Such investigation will allow us to comprehend the claim that the strategy of promoting political integration largely depends on the local intermediaries operating from different institutions, including religion. A thorough investigation of these dimensions will enrich the existing knowledge about the relationship between religion and civil society in relation to the process of addressing challenges of ethnic diversity, institutional collaboration, citizenship, and political integration. In exploring the viability of such a connection as well as unveil the prevailing challenges I propose to divide this exploration into three main parts, namely, the role of religion in public life, the relationship between religion and civil society, and the impact of pastoral letters and local churches on civil society.

Religion in Public Life

Many people, especially the youth, are becoming skeptical about the role of religion in public life. Young people are aware that most of the destructive conflicts have been fomented by people who profess one faith or another. In many ways, religious institutions have very often failed to uphold their prophetic role. We have to acknowledge that a number of religious communities have, in certain situations, served as a source for peace or violence. There is no doubt that many religions reveal exclusionist attitude which result into a lack of respect for other faith traditions, which stifle imagination as well as limit people's capacity to transcend faith-based prejudices. Such a situation has tempted a number of critics to claim that we need to conduct an audit of how religious communities have been responding to ethnocentrism as well as prolonged conflicts in places like Somalia, Sudan, and elsewhere.

Experience shows that religion is an ambivalent reality containing within itself the power to destroy or liberate human beings. Experience of the sacred takes several forms. It may be an experience of the first order in which the sacred is encountered directly in an ecstatic moment of mystical union; or, it could be an experience of the second order in which the sacred is mediated through mystical experiences. Both types of religious experience are necessarily filtered through the faculties of perception, with all the limitations of comprehension it implies, and then interpreted within the symbolic frame of ritual.[3] Such dynamics reveal that religion discloses the sacred with limitation in its ability to fully comprehend what it discloses.

To argue that religion is ambivalent is not to underestimate its sacred character and potential to transform social relationships; rather, it is to admit that religion is limited insofar as it is also shaped by cultural dynamics which derive from the fact that there is a distance between the infinite God and the finite human being. Ambiguity characterizes religious experience because historical experience presents a series of interacting changes with unpredictable effects. Religious experience occurs within competing possibilities. The ambivalence arises as the human perception, which is imperfect, encounters the sacred. A challenge that ambiguity poses to religious believers is to interpret the changing world of diverse experiences by maintaining its relationship with God.[4] In search for a lasting solution to the aforementioned limitation, I wish to argue that it is inappropriate to impose religious beliefs and practices on everybody. All people, as required by the Universal Declaration of Human Rights,[5] deserve freedom to practice religious beliefs of their own choice provided that in doing so they do not violate the norms of public order.[6]

Religions, nevertheless, remarks Mark Juergemeyer, cannot be left alone; they need the temper of rationality that enlightenment values give to civil society.[7] Without such awareness religions could be used to promote sectarian interests. For Christianity, attitudes of intolerance and exclusion contradict the basic message of the gospel which is to build the kingdom of peace and justice. Religions become the source of conflict because of doctrinal dispute, competition to increase the number of followers, and politicization of religious identity. In the case of South Africa, for example, during the apartheid era, a number of churches were used as tools that could support the apartheid system in order to safeguard privileges of the white minority. Such proponents claimed that the minority white South Africans were God's elected people, and that segregation based upon color was God's will.[8] By making reference to this experience, I wish to argue, we learn that without prophetic voices religion could also be used as a tool of sustaining structures of exclusion, status quo, and interests of the privileged. It is worthy noting that when there is no prophetic voice within religions, the privileged could use them to serve sectarian interests. With such experience at hand, one could argue that religion influences social relationships in different ways depending on how we appeal to it.

Because of cultural relativism and ethical pluralism, whether we like it or not, most of us are destined to live in religiously mixed societies. For this reason, we have to find ways in which people can relate to one another peacefully. The model of a single religion for a single state cannot fit in the modern world. The temptation of imposing one religion on everybody is often advocated by those who believe that desperate measures are required to enforce the model of theocratic state. Religions, because of the aforementioned limitations, must be encouraged to challenge themselves. Religions should agree on promoting spiritualities that defend human dignity because justice and peace form a part of the basic teaching of religions. Religions should put an accent on promoting friendship instead of intolerance.[9] The dynamics of other institutions should retain their autonomy; but such autonomy should not attempt to exclude the role of religion from the public sphere.

There are three extreme positions that must be avoided whenever we appeal to religion to promote political transformation. The first position is the one that excludes religion from the public sphere. On this front, a number of scholars tend to enforce the idea that religion must be confined to the private sphere because it is irrational; and, while it could be tolerated in the private sphere, it should not be allowed to play any role in the public sphere. The second position is found among those who enforce the idea of forming theocratic states. What is at stake in this position is that it ignores religious pluralism, freedom of choice, and cultural difference. The approach of imposing religious beliefs on everybody remains problematic and dangerous at best. In the context of Eastern

Africa, from my viewpoint, this approach will only worsen the situation by increasing the number of conflicts and political disorder. The third position makes use of religion to achieve political objectives. This position is vulnerable because extremists can hijack the religious cause to serve sectarian interests. In order to avoid these extremes we have to move toward a state that would be inclusive of all religions.

Religious virtues are valuable in the public life because the process of building the attitude of mutual care requires an interiorized commitment. Processes of community building are based on the spirituality of social love rather than sectarian interest. Any effort geared toward developing this vision requires a conscious intent to promote a society founded upon fundamental values. This approach must be founded upon the dynamics of self-transformation of the human person who is committed to the common good. Such a commitment constitutes categories required for any developed ethics of political organization.

There is no doubt that a number of religious traditions require reform. Nevertheless, it is a mistake to articulate ambiguities and limitations of religion without considering the constructive role of religion in public life. Religious contributions, from the viewpoint of statecraft, are often ignored by local governments and foreign policy practitioners, which, if properly used, could be an incentive to the process of nation-building. Politicians and policymakers alike fail to recognize the role that religious peacemakers can play in building trust and facilitating processes of building a just political order. Opportunities lost include the joint application of religious and political virtues that could lead to a peaceful resolution of differences rather than a resort to violence.[10] With the claim that religion cherishes public values more strongly than any other institution makes it a credible partner in the process of political transformation. The task of building a just political order cannot be left to the political initiative alone; it also requires collaboration emerging from other institutions, including religion. The argument that I uphold here is that religious practices should be approached as a platform that reinforces the foundation of public morality. Such possibility derives from the fact that religious activities shape public conscience.

The role of religion in public life could win trust of the warring sides both at the personal and communal levels. Trust could be won through persuasion when those in conflict negotiate their differences. In this process, the role of religion serves as a bridge between social groups in supporting social interaction and mutual care. In the case of Mozambique, for example, religious leaders played the role of facilitating interaction between social groups by encouraging people at the grassroots level to support the peace process. Religious activities enhance friendship and solidarity. This is done by facilitating interactive process of sharing ideas and producing alternative solutions to social problems. Religious motivation facilitates the process of nurturing the communal identity and commitment. The use of different resources to advance public morality enriches the process of inclusion and mutuality. Religion provides alternative resource for moral discourse, and encourages participation by providing a space for communication and self-expression. Such a space provides a direct framework of informal network of interaction and dialogue.

One could also argue that a number of religions, in recent years, have emerged as a key player in social transformation. This kind of engagement could also be interpreted to include reshaping of multicultural expectations that make peaceful solutions possible because it goes beyond legal framework and political dispute. When dealing with conflicts, for example, it becomes necessary to move beyond formal channels of diplomacy in order to uncover as well as deal with the deeper sources that rebuild relationships as well as make the necessary adjustments wherever possible. In this context, reconciliation born of spiritual conviction can play a critical role in inspiring the parties in conflict to break the cycle of revenge that typically characterizes such disputes. At best, faith-based morality generates motivational support to the sense of obligation and service to the community. Such a process convenes religious virtues and civic virtues in the process of cultivating mutuality for the sake of the common good. The horizon of religious virtues transcends the dimension of self-interest. Spiritual imaginations and practices supply the missing link between virtue ethics and the transformation of moral habits. Dynamics of spirituality develop specific practices of worship and service meant to deepen engagement with God and community. Indirectly, these practices train imaginations and emotions to produce a way of life consonant with public morality. They, in turn, provide normative considerations that keep spiritual practices fruitful in promoting civic virtues. Unless we are engaged at the level of attitude and character formation we cannot be engaged at the level of socio-political transformation.

The public role of religion is not just to give public pronouncements, but rather to participate in the formation of public conscience that effects social practice. The formation of the public conscience and the task of influencing the formation of public policy draw religion into the task of conscience-building. The religious actors provide a useful resource that allows the political process to be enriched by religious values. A religious contribution enables political discourse to respond appropriately to the increased complexity of social relationships. As such, religious involvement must be conceived as a contribution to a larger political process to which all institutions contribute. From the perspective of this argument, a local parish has the potential to become a zone of mutual exchange and formation of responsible citizens. Preaching about God's righteousness prepares the ground for social transformation. Such a view of social transformation shows that religion can be politically engaged even if it has no political power. Each faith sharing session is, by implication, a public activity. The power of religion challenges all forms of injustice that work against the spirit of sharing. It is through such dynamics that religion becomes one of the forces of social transformation. With this knowledge about the role of religion, it is therefore an exaggeration to conclude, without reservation, that intolerance characterizes the nature of religion. Various forms of religiously motivated conflicts cannot persuade us to reject completely the role of religion in the public sphere. To exclude religion from the public sphere is in fact to misunderstand the dynamics of religion, thereby underestimating its ability to transform social structures. Religion possesses distinctive capacities to enhance participation and commitment. A reasonable involvement of religion in the public sphere can bring contributions that strengthen the sense of mutual care and public good. If religious communities bring a significant contribution to the public life, then their role in social transformation cannot be ignored.

In promoting a deeper meaning of life, religious practices strengthen social identity and commitment through the cultivation of virtues that reinforce solidarity. Although religions reveal divisive tendencies it is an exaggeration to deny the fact that some religious communities advocate inclusive understanding of civic life and the values required to enhance the common good. It is not true that all religions are always involved in fomenting conflicts. Such a sweeping statement is based on selective considerations of events of a few religious movements. It is a mistake to generalize the public role of religion. The characteristics of the most conflict-prone and exclusivist religious groups are certainly not universal attributes of religion as such. Many of the conflicts in the world today that have religious dimensions are not simply clashes between faiths; rather, religion is often a flag that serves as a rallying point for other politicized aspects of corporate identity and interest.

It is true that a number of religious communities rejected ideas of pluralism, human rights, and freedom of conscience; but today, on the contrary, a number of religious communities accept these ideals and participate actively in promoting civic life based on these values. The role of religion in public is justified by the fact that activities of religious communities reveal an inclusive understanding of the public values and the common good. Activities of some religious movements and commitment of some religious leaders demonstrate that there can be a constructive integration between faith and the public good. A good example could be drawn from the struggle of Archbishop Desmond M. Tutu to promote reconciliation in the post-apartheid South Africa. When suspicion overshadows goodness, examples of good works can easily be overlooked. Religious teachings, when applied properly, contribute in the process of building the fabric of the common good. It is not true that all religious activities overlook ideals of democracy, freedom, and pluralism. A number of religious activities strengthen values of participation and common good. Such horizon is pursued by strengthening public virtues and cultivating the spirit of mutual care. The role of religion in society is constructive insofar as it is able to raise issues of public interest that have eluded other institutions.

Religion can play a constructive role in public life insofar as we acknowledge that the role of religion in public life is limited, and as such it must always be subjected to self-examination and self-criticism. From organizational viewpoint, intolerance is a symptom of a much deeper problem that must be dealt with through the process of attitude and character formation. Mutuality is a process of reconstructing relationships between individuals, social groups, and communities. Such engagement involves the process of integrated roles, functions, and activities. Such engagement shows that spiritualities of mutual care offer what statecraft cannot offer.

Religious communities can directly support dynamics of democracy, justice, reconciliation, and solidarity. Through the paradigm of restorative justice religion surpasses legal and retributive dimensions of justice. Religious communities are able to oppose intolerance through inter-religious dialogues that can establish trust when dialogue partners perceive that they are not being dragged into doctrinal disputes.

The dynamics of religion maintains the balance between the individual and the society. Such a process occurs when there is a development of the mind, refinement of the spirit, and the strength of the body that lead to the reform of the individual, and this will lead to the betterment and strength of the society, since society consists of individuals and the building of a society depends on the quality of its citizens, and the strength of a society derives from the strength of its components. If one component is advanced at the expense of others, the resulting imbalance will affect the whole society. Appropriate approaches organize institutions in such way that there is a balance between all aspects of social life so that one institution does not dominate another, or attention is not given to one while neglecting another, or giving one institution privilege while depriving another. The social organization, at the realm of day-to-day interaction, must establish a balance between the spirit and the body; otherwise disorder would infiltrate the society, and thereby causing cracks that could appear in its structure even if the lawmakers attempt to remedy one aspect or another. There cannot be a balanced interaction between institutions without a framework that brings together civic virtues and religious virtues.[11] Such a convergence is indeed the link that I intend to explore in the discussion.

Given the diversity of beliefs, identities, and interests, what ground does one has to bring religious beliefs into public sphere? To answer this question we have to show how politics interact with religion without overriding principles of autonomy, distinction, and separation. Differently stated, politics and religion have a functional interaction while at the same time maintaining institutional separation. To maintain such relationship one needs adequate knowledge of how religion, ethnicity, and politics complement one another. The language that separates secular from the sacred dimension tends to create unnecessary dualism, and could be misleading. The principle of functional interaction and institutional separation is founded upon the claim that everything in existence is a multi-dimensional whole, which encompasses a variety of interactions between parallel component entities on each level and those between such entities belonging to different levels as well. Religions are invariably embedded into the fabric of public life, and thus an attempt to confine them to the private sphere would violate religious identities. So, one has to maintain the tension and seek the right balance between the two principles, which need to be affirmed simultaneously.

With regard to the model of engagement in public life, the formula of institutional separation and functional interaction justifies the claim that each institution is autonomous and possesses its own sources and methodologies of searching the truth. However, there is always a dimension of interconnection and interdependence between institutions. There is no institution that can claim to be completely separated from other institutions. As such, there must be a platform of mutual cooperation and mutual enrichment. Religion ought to learn how to contribute in the public discourse without reducing religion to politics and vice versa. A difficulty emerges when there are serious disagreements about where to draw the line of demarcation between religion and politics. Churches should see themselves as a part of the world endowed with capacity and obligation to participate in social transformation. If religion is to be taken seriously it must engage in dialogue with other institutions.

Although there is a general concern on how responsibly public religion's influence will be exercised, given fanatical and anti-democratic approaches that result from religious convictions, religious groups, nonetheless, cannot be withdrawn from public life. In order to achieve a healthy complementarity between religion and politics, a number of ethical principles must be respected. These principles include acknowledgement of pluralism, rational dialogue, tolerance, self-evaluation, and self-criticism. There is a need of inclusive public sphere in which individuals could debate and collectively decide on matters of common interest, including political organization and the framework of the common good. Religion is a motivating force that moulds human identity, conscience, and public morality. It includes not just those ideas, attitudes, and activities we call religion, but all the ways of thinking, interacting, and acting with respect to what we believe will ultimately become foundational to public values. On the other hand, political activity spells out fundamental values of the society by conducting the common search for the common good, promotion of justice and rights, participation, and human dignity. It regulates ethics of social relationships by promoting the welfare of the person, social life, distribution of goods, and other values underlying the dynamics of social relationships. Religion promotes self-cultivation, which is crucial for the formation of responsible citizens. Religion has a public role, and, as such, secularization is not the decline of religion itself, but the decline in religion's ability to influence other spheres of life.[12]

Religion and Civil Society

From a democratic viewpoint, civil society is defined as a sphere of collective interaction between social groups and institutions that facilitates participation. Civil society could also be defined as a sphere of self-governing associations dedicated to alleviating human suffering by promoting transformative education, healthcare movements, environmental protection, human rights, conflict resolution, and establishment of democratic institutions.[13] Such a broad definition covers a wide spectrum of institutions and activities ranging from different institutions, organizations, and social groups.[14] Components of civil society include private humanitarian agencies, charity organizations, church-related agencies, and human rights movements actively responding to the need to improve life conditions. Religious organizations have also become actors in the process of promoting democratic change in societies torn apart by political disorder. Their presence activates the whole spectrum of social change by bringing creative actors into the process of social change. Religion promotes stronger commitment and loyalty than other identities.

Ideals of democracy cannot be realized without a vibrant sphere of civil society. The structure of civil society is crucial for participation, creativity, and transformation because the acquisition and use of power "determine how political order is to be constructed and governed. It is at the deeper level of state reconstruction that the importance of the idea of civil society becomes apparent."[15] The structure of civil society is constituted by activities and social networks, which includes informal clubs, religious organizations, non-profit service providers, labor and trade unions, political action groups, mass media, and so forth. The dynamics of civil society operate between social groups, with characteristics of participation and localization. Such a characteristic justifies the claim that civil associations reside outside the formal governmental institutions. The role of civil society is not to replace the state, but to motivate participation, inclusion, creativity, and transformation.

Civil society, founded upon the principles of subsidiarity and participation, is a foundation of democracy, leadership, and good governance. It is an important part of the political process because it seeks to expand the platform of political participation by shaping public values, decisions, and policies. Associational life promotes creativity, alternative thinking, and creative participation. The sphere of civil society is concretized and localized through grassroots the self-organization of associations, which acts as a means to acknowledge pluralism of identity and interest that exist between social groups. Voluntary associations are different from political parties, which seek to acquire mandate from people to form a government.

The initiative to transform political organization stands in constant tension with the state. The role of civil society is not to replace the state, but to balance the use of power in the society. The objective of civil society is to promote an inclusive sphere of justice that requires a convergence of social activities, popular participation, and collective determination. According to Iris Marion Young, civil society promotes participation, freedom of choice, self-innovation, and the virtues of democracy. Some political commentators suggest that "civil society is better equipped than the state to meet needs, deliver services, and further social solidarity."[16] On this view, the power of the state should be restricted in order to allow the flourishing of associational life. Civil society enables the emergence of public sphere in which differentiated social sectors express their experience and formulate their opinions. Public sphere enables citizens to expose injustice and make the exercise of power accountable. Civil associations, as actors of civil society, enrich the formation process of an agreed-upon concept of the common good, catalyze institutional transformation by engaging associational activity, enhance participation from the grassroots level, and legitimize political representation. The platform of civil society expands the sphere of participation, creativity, and mutuality. The function of civil society could also be presented as a foundation of democracy because it facilitates the realization of civic virtues by stimulating the formation of public values underlying transformation of social relationships.

Civil associations are agents of political change and motivators of social groups demanding recognition of the activities leading toward integral development. The platform of civil associations, as stated above, is not intended to replace the state, but to shape social relationships. Civil associations and the state coexist in a complex relationship of creative tension. The former plays the role of power balance by challenging state hegemony. Such a framework challenges tendencies toward totalitarianism by the state. The process of democratization and political reform need organizational mediation that can play the role of building a social cohesion supported by all citizens rather than holding on political systems characterized by outdated ideologies and the cult of personality that have led to the spiral of civil wars. The state should be constantly checked by a plurality of self-organized and vigilant civil associations whose functions is to nurture basic rights, to advocate popular claims, and to educate citizens in the democratic arts of pluralism, tolerance, interdependence, and mutual accommodation.[17] This popular upsurge, for example, performs the role of pushing for political transition by ensuing consolidation of political democracy with the aim of building cohesive social organization. Such initiative produces a significant impact insofar as it can create a space for public debate. An engagement of this sort can promote alternative models of governance based upon accountability. Associational life serves as a basis for creativity and self-determination. These activities revitalize grassroots communities to develop alternative thinking and motivate people to take control of the conditions of life under which they live. It widens the space for public participation and social action.

The input of civic education at the grassroots level is a condition that guarantees political transformation. Intellectually empowered people would participate more creatively in the process of political transformation. Democracy is not just a matter of electing leaders during a general election; it is also about holding governments accountable, transformation of institutions and attitudes, and implementation of public policies. Intellectually empowered people would be in a position to challenge irresponsible leadership and abuse of power. Such expectations could be realized when people are knowledgeable and actively engaged in the process of evaluating strategies proposed for development. Adequate civic education in this regard will produce people who are favorable to democracy.

Investing in education encourages intellectual empowerment, creative participation, and competence. Formation of responsible citizens is crucial because the process of building a viable civil society takes time, and it evolves from the direct struggles of the people. Effective sphere of civil society emerges from the contestations of power, realignment of socio-political forces, and commitment of associations toward networking, creation of grounds for political participation, and creation of checks and balances of power.[18] The challenge of building social cohesion and political stability rests upon the shoulders of the people. The process of democratization can produce a constructive impact insofar as people are willing to establish comprehensive models of participation and decision-making. It is a process that entails resolute determination to empower organizations. The process must also be able to challenge the status quo and its custodians aiming to capture the state to protect sectarian interests.

Participatory activities can produce a significant impact when there is administrative set-up geared to provide an opportunity to devolve power to the grassroots. This approach is justified by the principle of subsidiarity. From the perspective of people-centered development, social mobilization programs motivate people to organize as well as to seek access to available opportunities and resources. There is no development effort that can succeed without participation of the people from the grassroots level. From the perspective of such an argument one could conclude that the process of democratization through political transformation cannot take place through a top-down approach. Political transformation requires multiple actors operating at different levels of social organization. The sphere of civil society can create a significant impact insofar as they can promote localized methodologies that put an accent on accountability to the local population instead of foreign agencies as it is the case among non-governmental organizations today. Such methodologies guarantee a space for dialogue, self-discovery, and creativity. The advantage that emerges from localized initiative is that it can respond quickly to specific situations as well as tailor programs that could fit local needs. Grassroots structures of leadership provide early warning about developing situations that can cause conflict in the future. Such awareness motivates the people concerned to propose effective programs of information exchange, participation, and action.

The point we have to retain from this analysis thus far in order to facilitate the discussion is that the relationship between religion and civil society derives from the fact that these institutions operate through the principles of subsidiarty and participation. These principles are fundamental in the process of moral formation of conscience, character, commitment, and social relationships. In order to contextualize the relationship between religion and civil society, as we have pointed out from the outset, I propose at this point to examine the impact of small Christian communities and pastoral letters on civil society from the perspective of the Catholic Church.

The Impact of the Local Church on Civil Society

Since the independence of Eastern Africa countries in the 1960s, the Catholic Church, for example, has devised three methodologies intended to localize the church, namely, inculturation of liturgy, small Christian communities, and pastoral letters.[19] In 1973, the Catholic bishops proposed small Christian communities to be given priority in all pastoral activities. For the bishops, the creation of the small Christian communities is a concrete realization of the communitarian model of being church in the modern world, a way that can transcend sectarianism, ethnocentrism, and hopelessness. During their Study Conference in Nairobi, Kenya, they declared:

> We are convinced that in these countries of Eastern Africa it is time for the church to become really "local," that is: self-ministering, self-propagating, and self-supporting. Our plan is aimed at building such local churches for the coming years. We believe that in order to achieve this we have to insist on building church life and work on basic Christian communities, in both rural and urban areas. Church life must be based on the communities in which everyday life and work takes place: those basic and manageable social groupings whose members can experience real interpersonal relationships and feel a sense of communal belonging, both in living and working. We believe that Christian communities at this level will be best suited to become effective witness in their natural environment.[20]

Later, in July 1976, the Catholic bishops held a plenary session focused on building small Christian communities in Eastern Africa.

This meeting evolved from the guidelines they recommended at their 1973 conference. On this occasion, they again stressed that the systematic formation of small Christian communities should be the pastoral priority in the years to come within their region.[21]

The Catholic bishops opted for small Christian communities because of the following reasons: to inculturate the Christian faith with the hope of promoting socio-political transformation, traditional values of solidarity, and to carry out a transition from a paternalistic church to a mature church governed by indigenous Christians. They believed that the relatively small size of such Christian communities would enable members to relate to one another more easily. Pastoral experience has shown that the model of small Christian communities challenges the individual not only to confront the changing world around oneself, but also to assume a total commitment to religious virtues and involvement in shaping social conditions of life. This approach also aimed at forming groups of Christians living in social proximity to enable them to know each other well. Such approach, if well developed, could also inspire the idea of civil society operating under the principle of subsidiarity.

With such a background, it is appropriate to demonstrate the relationship between the dynamics of small Christian communities and civil society. Small Christian communities and civil society converge in realizing some of their intended goals because both of them uphold principles of subsidiarity, participation, localization, and common good. Such a functional convergence is extended to the task of promoting human rights and social justice. After making the link between bishops' pastoral letters and small Christian communities on civil society, we now turn to the impact of the pastoral letters on civil society.[22]

The Catholic bishops, through pastoral letters, have occasionally challenged political decisions that appear detrimental to the common good. Concerning the impact of bishops' pastoral letters, a number of Christians claim that denouncing and condemning social evils is important, but on its own is not enough. The Catholic bishops of Kenya, for example, have partially succeeded in delivering a promising teaching on values of democracy, social justice, and political reform, and the need for Christian engagement in promoting these values.[23] They advocated a revision of the National Constitution of Kenya because, in preparation for independence, the national constitution was formulated by a few individuals in an *ad hoc* manner and without the full participation of the people. Such national constitutions need revision and endorsement by a popular consent. They argue that a complete revision of the national constitutions must be entrusted to a large constituent body of experienced and competent citizens representing all institutions, communities, and associations. In addition to that bishops have raised a prophetic voice against corruption, ethnocentrism, and conflict.

Since the Second Vatican Council, five decades ago, the Catholic Church has really become a major actor in the public life of many countries. It exerts pressure toward democracy through its social teaching and leadership.[24] It has provided support, protection, and leadership for popular opposition movements challenging irresponsible leadership. This effort represents a major shift in the identity and self-understanding of the Catholic Church throughout the world. The obligation to participate in shaping the moral character of society is a requirement of Christian ethics. The religious obligation is rooted in Christian commitment to bear Christian witness in all we do. It is necessary that all Christians participate in promoting the common good. The Catholic social teaching teaches that all citizens should play an active role in public life.[25] In many ways, the Catholic action models have tended to integrate themselves into existing structures. In so doing the aim has been, first, to train highly qualified people deeply familiar with the social teaching of the church. Then these people should insert themselves into existing social structures, the idea being that they can shape and guide social institutions in accord with social teaching of the church. Pastoral action ought to focus on promoting social justice and human rights. Social ministry aims at action that leads to social change. Such ministry is inherently political and involves pastoral strategies whose aim is the social change of the institutions and systems that govern society.

Prevailing Challenges

The two examples briefly examined above, small Christian communities and pastoral letters, provide a framework that could be used to link religion and civil society. The existence of the two methodologies does not, however, overcome a number of difficulties related to the relationship between religion and politics. At this junction of the discussion I propose to outline a number of concrete factors that make the effort of linking activities of religion to civil society in the process of addressing social issues difficult.

Most often, when Catholic bishops speak out through pastoral letters and occasional statements, reactions that emerge from political leaders and other churches tend to water down the message. A common reaction is that religions must refrain from interfering in politics, and instead, they should confine themselves to spiritual matters. Other churches tend to contradict the bishops' message because they do not have similar approaches toward political life. Instead of addressing political problems prevalent in the region, some of these churches concentrate on competing to increase the number of followers and religious supremacy.

The challenge for African churches is not situated on the level of the teaching itself, but on the lack of effective methodologies of implementation. For instance, a number of church directives tend to confine themselves to pronouncements, such as the need for justice and peace without engaging in initiatives geared to promote social change. My argument is that theoretical information without action-oriented strategies produces insignificant impact on the ground. It is time to build alternatives, not only to denounce. The prevailing situation in Eastern Africa countries needs more than a teaching confined to the pulpit. It needs centers designed for the formation of public conscience and social action. Such initiative must be accompanied with trained personnel who can reach people in their families, working places, small Christian communities, and other activities of social interaction beyond the parish building. Church leaders must first of all listen to the voices of the people who are mostly affected by poverty at the grassroots level before they triumphantly proclaim themselves as the voice of the voiceless. Such a demand requires church leadership to be concretely engaged in promoting skills required for linking religious virtues to civic virtues. Christians need information and formation for personal growth and commitment toward political transformation.

For critics, methodologies of small Christian communities and pastoral letters have a limited echo among ordinary people because they do not provide methodologies for transmitting information and formation of the people concerned. The language used in these letters is very often an obstacle to the spreading of the message. Some of these letters are written in a language that cannot be grasped very easily by ordinary people, and they sometimes appear to be influenced by doctrinal disputes. Similarly, the language used reflects a top-down approach in organization and administration. My argument is that if these letters were written in a pragmatic language, their message could easily be understood by ordinary people and thereby create an impact at the level of family, parish, faith-sharing groups, and church-related associations.

Pastoral letters must be prepared in collaboration with lay professionals. They have to be people-driven as well as focus on building effective institutions rather than changing a given regime and individual. There must be informed personnel able to read the signs of the times in advance in order to alleviate crises. This is an important reminder because reactions from churches tend to emerge when it is too late. Such a task requires people who are well-formed in the knowledge of leadership, governance, and ethics of the common good. Such formation will eventually become a reality insofar as people are able to construct a strong relationship between spirituality and politics.

From an inter-institutional viewpoint, one could argue that there is no active collaboration between church-related associations and secular institutions in matters pertaining to social transformation. The reason is that the issue of institutional collaboration has not been taken seriously, and it is often obscured by endless competition geared to increase the number of followers. The condition in which their followers live is not a point of concern at all. My argument is that evangelization cannot be limited to handing on the faith in the form of doctrine, as it has tended to be; rather, it has to be a dialogue between the lives of the people and the message of the gospel in such a way that people find strength to encounter the challenge of life. A number of religious leaders speak about the need to promote dialogue, but they are very slow to put such rhetoric into practice. This situation arises because the hierarchy is too rigid and hardly learns from the experience of others. The lack of dialogue between religions and secular institutions, I wish to argue, makes the pastoral letters insignificant. My conclusion is that if there is no collaboration between institutions in promoting social justice, human rights, and the common good, the pastoral letters will have an insignificant impact in public life.

During the time of crisis, apparently, a number of church institutions tend to be silent as well as indifferent as though there is nothing wrong. And when they react it is often too late. This is not a

110

condemnation, but a matter of fair examination of conscience. It is true that sometimes a crisis may be so deep that churches are not able to act directly. In such a situation, however, churches can play the role of appealing to the public conscience. Churches should not wait until there is full blown war; instead, they should point out what is happening while the conditions for conflict are developing, because it may become too late to prevent open conflict, and the means to act could also become limited. It is inappropriate for Christians to preoccupy themselves with doctrinal disputes while failing to address concrete challenges of social life.

A number of church leaders are afraid to challenge ineffective governments because they are integrated into the partisan politics. Such situation compels them to prefer diplomacy. But, diplomacy without clear objectives to pursue could be interpreted as a means to avoid the demands of justice. The liberating power of God cannot be realized in history without human involvement. It is God who takes the initiative, but human beings must respond to make it a reality in history.

African churches are also called to reform spiritualities that tend to make a separation between the sacred and the secular dimensions of human experience. This weakness derives from the lack of clear spirituality and methodology of political engagement, transformation, and advocacy. This attitude, by extension, derives from the understanding that we are only pilgrims on the earth, and as such ideas of social transformation are irrelevant to Christians. Such understanding has also strengthened the claims of complete separation between religion and politics. The second area of concern derives from the partisan politics. The fact is that we do not have clear methodologies of approaching political issues. We tend to support political parties without a clear vision. This is because we tend to support political ideologies that sustain sectarian interest fashioned by ethnic affiliation and social class. Such a position renders religious leaders irrelevant during the period of political crises. The third weakness derives from the inadequate skills of exercising principles of subsidiarity and localization. The fourth weakness is related to religious competition, religious pluralism, and diplomacy which tend to overshadow the public role of churches because secrecy overlooks the rights of participation. The fifth challenge is that civil society tends to exclude private dimensions of individual and family life, the input of religious virtues, and contribution of the church-related organizations seeking to win a formal place within the public sphere and state power infrastructure. The sixth challenge that must be addressed is whether or not churches are part of the civil society. If one would contend with the fact that churches' activities have political consequences which in essence do not surrender the ontological content of the intended message, then surely churches are functionally part of and at the same time distinct from civil society.[26] The aforementioned weaknesses and challenges suggest that African churches must redefine their public role and institutional collaboration in order to be in a position of promoting the common good.

With regard to the weaknesses of non-governmental organizations, I wish to argue that a number of them are created to raise funds for private use instead of promoting political reform and formation of responsible citizens. Such situation has rendered non-governmental organizations accountable to foreign organizations instead of the local population. Consequently they maintain the practice of irresponsible leadership prevalent in the public institutions.[27] As such, the sphere of civil society cannot flourish when it is flooded by people and organizations geared to promote partisan interests. If we do not focus on overcoming these weaknesses, both, church-related agencies and non-governmental organizations will create insignificant impact in the process of social transformation and formation of responsible citizens.

Conclusion

With regard to local initiatives and methodologies of institutional collaboration, the following questions could guide us toward concrete engagement, advocacy, and implementation of creative ideas. First, what resources do religious communities need to become effective agents of social transformation? Second, which models of collaboration between religion and other agents of civil society seem to be effective? Third, can religion and other agents of civil society work together for the sake of the common good? Any effort geared to answer these questions should be welcomed because religions, as clearly stated in the discussion, are often seen by agents of civil society as sectarian and divisive. The central point to these questions is that one institution, on its own, cannot regulate all dimensions of human life. Following the same rationale one could conclude that Christian mission cannot be carried out successfully in isolation.

Complementarity between institutions is necessary for integral development of a human person. One could argue that methodologies of promoting social justice and human rights through local churches have created insignificant impact in public life due to the lack of centers designed for formation, political activism, institutional collaboration, and social action. Such challenges compel us to device new ways that can shape the future through engagement at the grassroots level and research projects that can promote social activism.

The discussion introduced the dimensions of interaction and complementarity between institutions into the process of public morality and the need of assessing all possibilities surrounding questions involving the relationship between religious conscience and political responsibility. The art of combining prophetic vision and political wisdom bears fruits in recognizing interdependence between institutions. In the process of forming a cohesive society, neither secular humanism nor religious doctrine is privileged. We are expected to leave behind mentalities of sectarianism, imposition, exclusion, and authoritarianism. In the modern world we are living in complex socio-political realities where people of different cultures, religions, and interests are mixed up. We cannot live in harmony without embracing virtues of tolerance, dialogue, and equal citizenship. In addition, we have to acknowledge that a balance between institutions is a foundation of democratic citizenship. Such confirmation endorses the claim that to exclude religion from the public sphere would obstruct avenues of experience by excluding certain institutions from sharing their experience toward the process of building inclusive public morality. Every individual, group, and institution has a right and duty to participate in the process of shaping the political process as a means of promoting the well-being of every person, group, and community. Formation of effective institutions requires commitment toward social justice, equal citizenship, and collaboration. Without embracing these values we cannot overcome the challenges of ethno-political competition, discrimination, and conflict.

Notes

[1] For further elaboration, see the works of David Hollenbach, S.J., *The Global Face of Public Faith: Politics, Human Rights, and Christian Ethics* (Washington, D.C.: Georgetown University Press, 2003); *The Common Good and Christian Ethics* (Cambridge, Massachusetts: Cambridge University Press, 2002); Ian S. Markham, *Plurality and Christian Ethics* (Cambridge, Massachusetts: Cambridge University Press, 1994).

[2] A good example could be drawn from the complaint presented in the *Daily Nation, Kenya* by John Ngirachu and Oliver Mathenge, "Don't Kill Our Reform Dream, Church Urged," *Daily Nation, Kenya* (April 5, 2010): 1, 4. Some Christian churches, according to these authors, have become a hindrance to reform by introducing forcefully doctrinal disagreements on abortion to the national constitutional debates. Other religions concentrate on the temptation of including religious code in the national constitution. These attitudes portray religion as a hindrance toward the effort of promoting political integration and mutual accommodation.

[3] R. Scott Appleby, *The Ambivalence of the Sacred: Religion, Violence, and Reconciliation* (New York: Rawman and Littlefield, 2000), 29.

[4] Ruth Page, *Ambiguity and the Presence of God* (London: SCM, 1985), 1.

[5] United Nations, *Universal Declaration of Human Rights*, 1948, Articles 1, 18.

[6] Avery Dulles, S.J., "Christ Among the Religions," *America* (May, 2000): 14.

[7] Mark Juergensmeyer, *Terror in the Mind of God: The Global Rise of Religious Violence* (Berkeley, California: University of California Press, 2000), 243.

[8] Carl Niehaus, "Reconciliation in South Africa: Is Reconciliation Relevant?" in James Cochrane, John de Gruchy, and Stephen Martin, eds., *Facing the Truth: South African Faith Communities and the Truth and Reconciliation Commission* (Cape Town: David Philip Publishers Limited, 1999), 81-90, at 85.

[9] Michael Amaladoss, "Religions for Peace," *America* (December 10, 2001): 6-8, at 8.

[10] Douglas M. Johnston, Jr., "Religion and Foreign Policy," in Raymond G. Helmick, S.J., and Rodney L. Petersen, eds., *Forgiveness and Reconciliation: Religion, Public Policy, and Conflict Transformation* (Philadelphia: Templeton Press, 2001), 117-128, at 120.

[11] Integration of religious virtues and civic virtues is fully discussed by Robert Audi and Nicholas Wolterstorff, *Religion in the Public Square: The Place of Religious Convictions in Political Debate* (New York: Rowman and Littlefield Publishers, 1997), 25-55; Richard John Neuhaus, *The Naked Public Square: Religion and Democracy* (Michigan: William B. Eerdmans Publishing Company, 1984).

[12] Robert Wuthnow, *Christianity and Civil Society: The Contemporary Debate* (Valley Forge, Pennsylvania: Trinity Press International, 1996), 17, 26.

[13] It is appropriate to note that civil society is not synonymous to non-governmental organizations.

[14] Pamela Aall, "What Do Non-Governmental Organizations Bring to Peacemaking?" in Chester A. Crocker, Fen Osler Hampson, and Pamela Aall, eds., *Turbulent Peace: The Challenges of Managing International Conflict* (Washington, D.C.: United States Institute of Peace Press, 2001), 365-383, at 367.

[15] John W. Harbeson, "Civil Society and Political Renaissance in Africa," in John W. Harbeson, Donald Rothchild, and Naomi Chazan, eds., *Civil Society and the State in Africa* (Boulder, Colorado: Lynne Rienner Publishers, 1994), 1-29, at 10.

[16] Iris Marion Young, *Inclusion and Democracy* (Oxford: Oxford University Press, 2000), 155.

[17] Michael Bratton, "Civil Society and Political Transitions in Africa," in Harbeson, Rothchild, and Chazan, eds., *Civil Society and the State in Africa*, 51-81, at 54.

[18] Julius O. Ihonvbere, *Economic Crisis, Civil Society, and Democratization: The Case of Zambia* (Asmara: Africa World Press, 1996), 270-271; John W. de Gruchy and Stephen William Martin, eds., *Religion and the Reconstruction of Civil Society* ((Pretoria: University of South Africa, 1995), 22-60.

[19] On this section I opt to take the examples of pastoral letters and small Christian communities from the Catholic Church, within the context of Eastern Africa, as a way of concretizing the discussion. It is not my intention to exclude other churches and religions.

[20] AMECEA Study Conference, "Planning for the Church in Eastern Africa in 1980s," *AFER* 16, 1 (February, 1974): 1-32, at 10.

[21] On evolution of small Christian communities in Eastern Africa countries, see AMECEA Plenary Conference, "Building Christian Communities in Eastern Africa," *AFER*, 18, 5 (October, 1976).

[22] The analysis that I wish to present here is simply intended to point out areas of improvement, not to overlook the contribution of the pastoral letters and Catholic social teaching at large.

[23] See, for example, Pastoral Letters of the Catholic Bishops of Kenya, *On the Road to Democracy* (Nairobi: St. Paul Publications, 1994); *Our Social Responsibility* (Nairobi: St. Paul Publications, 1996).

[24] For verification, see Pastoral Letters of the Catholic Bishops of Kenya compiled by Rodrigo Mejia, S.J., ed., *The Conscience of Society* (Nairobi: St. Paul Publications, 1995).

[25] Austin Flannery, ed., *The Second Vatican Council: The Conciliar and Post-Conciliar Documents, Gaudium et Spes*, No. 76.

[26] Nicholas Otieno, *Human Rights and Social Justice in Africa* (Nairobi: All Africa Conference of Churches, 2007), 82-91.

[27] See, for example, the study made by Wolfgang Shonecke, "NGOs Making Business With People's Poverty," *New People*, 72 (May-June, 2001): 4-6; Aquiline Tarimo, S.J., "Human Rights and Democracy in Africa: The Role of Non-Governmental Organizations," *Sedos* (October, 2001): 262-269.

6. Foundations of Political Integration

At this juncture of the study it is appropriate to identify moral principles underlying the process of building a cohesive political society. The lesson we have learnt from ethnic competition and conflict is that an ordered society cannot be established without taking into account the values that hold local communities together. The initiatives already undertaken to correct the situation have encountered numerous difficulties, including the challenge of forming an agreed upon concept of the common good. Such a situation has rendered the process of political integration problematic. The situation arises from the fact that there are no political institutions within the continent of Africa that can govern people of different ethnic identities peacefully.

The rise of political movements for liberation, five decades ago, seems to have lost the ground of shaping the future. Movements of socialism, humanism, negritude, and authenticity have all created insignificant impact. After these grueling years of ideological movements came the rise of religious movements. These movements focused on religious expansion instead of integral development, thereby ending-up in failure in the struggle of shaping the future. The proliferation of non-governmental organizations, in a similar fashion, seems to have aggravated the situation of underdevelopment due to the lack of transformative strategy founded upon the ethics of responsible leadership and good governance.

The focus of this chapter is to unveil ethical foundations underlying the process of political integration. The import of these foundations, as a part of a wider socio-political process, situates the process of political integration beyond the scope of ethnic politics. The intended objective is to justify the claim that democracy is an attitude of mind, and, as such, democratic ideals cannot be realized when the formation of conscience, attitude, and character are taken for granted. There is no any other possibility that ideals of democracy could be realized apart from becoming culture. The discussion begins by presenting ethical foundations of public values upon which the meaning of self-determination, participation, accountability, and public good derive. Such a platform allows the discussion to demonstrate the relationship between public conscience and public reason. Another dimension considered in the discussion is the process of building public consensus through the convergence of religious virtues and civic virtues anchored upon a two-font principle of moral reasoning, namely, imagination and creativity.

Foundations of Public Values

The legitimacy of public values is founded upon four moral principles, namely, human dignity, freedom of conscience, human rights, and the common good. These principles challenge the dimension of diversity and seek to transcend the difficulties it creates by appealing to values that cut across different cultures and institutions. They form an integral whole for communication, engagement, and sharing without overriding the distinctive nature of each dimension of human experience.

Human dignity could be defined as an inherent worth of a human person. The concept of human dignity is widely regarded as a foundation for the claims of human rights, freedom of conscience, and the common good. The justification given for human dignity rests upon the claim that there is a permanent relation between a human being and God.[1] In this bond, human dignity is founded upon the value that brings together humanity and divinity. Ancient moral thinkers considered human dignity as a value deriving from the divine nature. Reason provides the basis for the understanding of human dignity, thereby providing foundation for the Universal Declaration of Human Rights. The same understanding informed various bills of rights, which came into existence before the *Declaration des Droits de L'homme et du Citoyen* of 1789.

From a political viewpoint, human dignity possesses authority over state sovereignty because a state is created to promote human dignity. From a religious perspective, the scripture teaches that human beings are created in the likeness and image of God. Such a teaching, from the book of Genesis, confirms the claim that a human being is sacred and end-in-himself. Although human beings are naturally tainted by sin, the image of God in them is considered to be a permanent attribute upon which human dignity is founded. An appeal to human dignity provides the basic premise for the understanding of human rights, whether they are conceived in civil-political or socio-economic terms. The divine attribute makes human dignity sacred and inalienable. To this end, human dignity has become a standard measure of social relationships and political institutions.

The second foundation of public values is freedom of conscience. Liberal democracy is resolute in defending human freedom. Its proponents believe that respect for human dignity cannot be possible without taking seriously human freedom. It presents human freedom as an ingredient that guarantees self-realization, self-esteem, and creativity. The involvement of an individual in the process of socialization enables the person to develop deliberate powers as well as the sense of purpose that result into a fully developed personality. Freedom of individuals is crucial for self-realization because some traditions and institutions tend to suppress alternative thinking, innovation, and creativity. The movement of enlightenment came as a gift to rescue people from aggressive uniformity. Experience shows that certain traditions can stifle human spirit from creativity, especially when they enforce fatalism and paternalism as God-given norms. The platform of freedom is not just the absence of limitations, but an impetus to do the right thing.

The third moral principle widely considered as a foundation of public values is human rights. Human rights could be defined as entitlements endowed to every human being by the virtue of being human. They are, by ethical standard, intrinsic and inviolable. They are founded upon sacred attributes that cannot be given by culture, and as such they must be respected, protected, and promoted. Justifications derive from the understanding that a human being is sacred and as such his worth is elevated beyond any other good. Such a description provides human rights a legitimacy of being recognized as foundational to public values. Human rights are referred to as standard norms that stand to judge every person, community, and institution. In the modern world, the criteria of human rights are the most reliable standard measure of any human conduct.

The recognition of human rights derives from the claim that they are founded upon fundamental values. It is these values that make human rights legitimate, universal, and normative. Human rights, as moral entitlements, are necessarily linked to the fundamental values. Claims of validity depend also on the moral agents who act within their context of life and the value system they inhabit.[2] From the perspectives of origin and evolution, the ethics of human rights emerged from socio-cultural, economic, and political transformations. They have relevance wherever there is injustice irrespective of culture, religion, or place. They seek to allow human beings to give meaning to their lives as well as pursue their own vision of the good life.[3] Such a function justifies the claim that freedom of conscience deserves respect. Human rights are legitimate moral norms because they present human dignity, self-determination, and the common good as necessary conditions for human flourishing.

Human rights, argues Ignacio Ellacuria, should be understood as the unfolding of the common good.[4] For him, human rights and the common good are a single problem. It is impossible to speak of a common good where there is a denial of human rights. The common good is that point where rights and duties converge to reinforce one another. When human rights are ignored, and when the pursuit of individual interests unjustly prevails over the common good, then the seeds of injustice are sown.[5] Human rights and the common good are mutually correlative, and specify the minimum standards required for a society that is just. Without the link proposed by Ellacuria human rights could be interpreted as a principle of self-protection expressed in terms of non-interference.

Realization of human rights, as a struggle for mutual recognition, is the sole paradigm in which fundamental disagreements are dissolved. Francis Fukuyama, in his book *The End of History and the Last Man*, takes seriously the possibility of using the criteria of human rights to judge the conduct of individuals, groups, and institutions.[6] He is correct in the claim he makes saying that history shows no better way to limit the power of state apart from using the criteria of human rights. The standards of human rights have become the most effective moral criteria to judge individuals, groups, and institutions.[7] Though there is no unanimity about the philosophical foundations of human rights, they provide an agreed upon platform for protecting and enhancing dignity of persons facing unfair treatment. Human rights standards have acquired international recognition because of the influence they have garnered since the end of the Second World War. Conversely, diversity and misunderstanding among value systems and meanings of the good life do not present another option that could be considered just and accepted by everybody. Under these circumstances it could be argued that human rights are the sole paradigm in which fundamental disagreements are dissolved. In search for a common morality there are no other respectable alternatives to human rights standards.

The fourth foundation of public values is the common good. Common good is defined as the sum total of social conditions that allow people, either as individuals or groups, to attain their fulfillment.[8] This definition necessitates the need to examine the way we relate to one another. The pursuit of happiness is more than a pursuit of self-gratification. Service for the community, political participation, and respect of diversity are the required ingredients for the formation of a meaningful citizenship.

The realization of the framework of the common good must be worked out in the context of each society. The reason is that there is an inescapable contextual dimension to any genuine understanding of the common good. The demand of the common good is the requirement to seek, form, and maintain political community. The common good is an experience of life among people who are determined to pursue common objectives through the performance of common actions.[9] The framework of the common good represents a good of society that transcends private interest. As such, the common good is not simply the sum total of individual interests; rather, it is a good that is common. The politics of the common good takes on a wider significance than simply the challenge of balancing the conflict of interests.[10] In this case, indeed, politics becomes the art of organizing identities, loyalties, and interests to achieve greater good. That is to say the art of socio-political organization involves taking into account different aspects of human experience.

The emphasis on the role of the common good in the process of building cohesive society requires us to develop unity that takes seriously cultural diversity. It is imperative to discourage unity that imposes uniformity in the interest of social order, and instead promote unity that promotes creativity in the interest of moral good.[11] A good life is founded upon the goods shared with others, the common good of the larger society of which one is a part. A good life for a single person and the quality of the common life persons share with others in community are necessarily interconnected. Following the same argument we can conclude that the good of the individual and the common good are inseparable.[12] There is always an indispensable interdependence between the good of the individual and the community.

The platform of the common good provides a conceptual organizing principle that mediates excesses of both individualism and communitarianism. It serves as a way of construing the relationship of the individual to a society so that the limits and possibilities of both individual and communal well-being are preserved, and in which the appropriate responsibilities that exist among individuals are defined and articulated.[13] With individualism, it puts an accent on the need to limit individual freedom; with communitarianism, it shares the conviction that only in the community context can the possibilities of flourishing for the individual be realized. Concepts of individual and community must be balanced in order to promote the platform of the common good. Such understanding requires us to be critical of closed communitarianism and individualism. These extremes lead to the destruction of the individual and the community. Citizens of a well-ordered society have final ends in common, including the ends of supporting institutions as well as give one another justice accordingly. The end of political justice must be conceived conceptually as well as practically so that citizens can give one another justice not merely by recognizing immunities from interference, but by acknowledging mutual interest in promoting the basic rights and obligations of serving each other. As such, the common good is the end of the public reason. Such confirmation supports the claim that common good is neither reduced to the personal interests of the individual nor super-imposed on the community. The common good is guaranteed when rights and duties are balanced and maintained.[14]

The framework of the common good provides the basis of building cohesive political society. The process of building the framework of the common good cultivates virtues in search for a common ground that can justly regulate identities, loyalties, and interests. Ordered political life entails commitment from individuals and groups to a program of ordered life grounded in mutuality. In the spirit of good citizenship, all members accept the responsibility toward the common good. The virtue of citizenship upholds the values of interdependence and communal responsibility.

Human dignity, freedom of conscience, human rights, and the common good are inextricably interconnected. None of these variables can be accurately comprehended without making reference to the others. Human dignity is the foundation of the freedom of conscience and human rights, which in turn actualize the worth of the human person. Given the fact that human dignity, freedom of conscience, and human rights cannot be realized in a vacuum, communal relationships become the context in which these values are realized, which, in the end necessitate the dimension of the common good. Ellacuria makes it clear when he argues that the promotion of the common good cannot progress by over-looking the challenge of promoting human dignity, freedom of conscience, and human rights, precisely because the process of promoting these values is an integral part of the common good.[15] That is to say human dignity, freedom of conscience, and human rights acquire their concreteness in the concept of the common good.

The ethical principles unveiled in the discussion are widely recognized as foundations of public values able to guide moral judgment and public discourse. These principles, from the viewpoint of political ethics, are recognized as civic virtues. Such influence has made them acquire international recognition and moral authority to the extent that they inspire formulation of public policies, ethics of good governance, and democratic accountability. They are no longer in contention at the level of public morality and international politics; rather, they are widely accepted because they are foundational and trans-cultural.[16] With such credibility these principles have ultimately become ethical foundations of public values, normative, and authoritative in public morality.

Participation and Accountability

From what has been said it begins to emerge that without due emphasis on fundamental values, the dynamics of political organization could easily be overwhelmed by sectarian interest. Civic responsibility is founded upon fundamental values that require everybody to be accountable to the community. Such a moral demand generates unceasing pressure on human sense of responsibility. People who have no sense of moral responsibility do not consider the consequence of their actions. Instead, they are only committed to the drive of satisfying immediate needs. Such people could be categorized as persons who are unable to practice the virtue of accountability.

A culture of responsible governance and democratic accountability emerge when people are able to organize the public sphere rationally. Such a process depends on the effort geared to sustain political structures able to contest the abuse of power by holding political leaders accountable to the people they lead. The emergence of the spirit of democratic accountability and good governance depends on the process of empowering the masses at the grassroots level, because democratic accountability, as a device for devolving power, refers not only to the political institutions, but also to the spirit that animates those institutions. A model of political organization that is not informed by conscience and reason degenerates into apathy and anarchy.[17]

Participatory democracy is a political framework designed for organizing public exercise of power in such way that it can facilitate participation in the process of decision-making for the benefit of all. It also concerns the procedure of reasoned deliberation among individuals considered as equal citizens. Effective principles of governance are established through rational dialogue that puts an accent on public reason and consensus. Participation, dialogue, and public reason play a crucial role in the practice of democracy. These principles produce a significant impact when they penetrate the dynamics of social relationships.

Having presented ethical foundations of public values I propose to turn to another set of ethical principles considered to be indispensable in the process of promoting political integration, namely, public conscience and public reason. The horizon of these principles is widely considered to be a platform upon which authority of public values derive.

Public Conscience and Public Reason

Conscience is defined as a centre of authority inherent in each person that entails respect for human freedom and autonomy. It is considered to be a forum of moral authority because it regulates the process of accounting for one's moral responsibility. The freedom of conscience plays a role of making people morally responsible in the process of discernment and decision-making. The authority of conscience empowers people to challenge disordered attitude, character, and behavior. Informed conscience makes a person a responsible moral agent. Such empowerment enables moral agents to respect opinion of others as well as promote creative thinking.

From a theological viewpoint, conscience could be defined as a sacred ground upon which a person exercises freedom. It could also be described as a sanctuary where a person becomes self-conscious. Functionally, the power of conscience refers to the dutiful obedience to what could be described as a divine voice speaking within us. These definitions confirm the claim that we are morally required to advocate the primacy of conscience. With regard to authenticity, the conscience of an individual is independent. The conscience of every person is sacred, unique, and autonomous. It is the most secret core of a person. At the level of conscience we are alone with God whose voice echoes in us.[18] Though we respect authority of institutions, we are also compelled to accord primacy to the conscience of an individual. The authenticity of conscience is a complete antithesis to tyranny. The recognition of its inviolability protects human being from disrespect, domination, and abuse. It does so to defend human dignity, freedom, and autonomy. Conscience is a moral capability that makes a human person a moral agent.

Freedom of conscience is independent and free from coercion. Such claim is crucial because sometimes institutional authority tends to infringe the exercise of one's freedom. Conscience, as a supreme power of one's dignity, deserves protection. Respect for a person's conscience, where the image of God is reflected, confirms the claim that we can only propose the truth to others; to impose on others what one considers to be the truth is an offense against human dignity and God whose image that person bears.[19] The conscience of each person must, however, be informed, formed, and function to promote fundamental values. Following one's conscience is more than obeying the law. Acting in conformity with one's conscience is the way in which people become responsible. The attributes of informed and formed conscience are crucial in the process of decision-making.

Public conscience, which derives from the conscience of individuals, is informed by a judgment of reason and moral evaluation of oneself and community with full commitment to what is right. It is a moral awareness within the heart of every person urging us to do what is right.[20] We have a responsibility to discern how to respond to compelling social issues, but we cannot differ on moral obligation to build a just world through morally acceptable means so as to defend human dignity. Such understanding helps us not to compromise the basic moral principles. In public life we practice the virtue of justice as a means of defending fundamental values that sustain the framework of the common good.

The dynamics of public conscience brings into play the virtues of loyalty and responsibility. However, the challenge emerges when a believer thinks that the laws of one's state are incompatible with the demands of one's religion. Such a challenge must be examined carefully, because a number of believers tend to think that religious practices must be part of the public policies. Such a situation generates tension in the conscience of the believer and public discourse. What could be recognized as lawful by lawmakers could be immoral from a religion viewpoint. For Thomas Shannon, the criterion of selective obedience provides a framework that people need to use at a given moment and context to be morally responsible persons.[21] A selective obedience provides a right for the moral agent to choose which law to obey, and the standard measure is the rightness of the conscience. Such a right is supported by the assumption that there is a higher law that ought to be obeyed.

Thomas Shannon, to clarify the matter, argues that the problem underlying the political discourse include the challenge of which order should make ultimate claims for obedience and loyalty from the believer. Such a challenge underscores the concept of selective obedience, which should be obeyed first, civil authority or religious authority, and under what circumstance? In search for an appropriate answer, the authority of conscience becomes central in the process of enabling the individual to challenge conditions that obstruct the exercise of freedom. Conscience is the ultimate norm of morality that regulates the dynamics of public life. It has to be considered as an authentic criterion for judging the conduct of individuals, groups, and institutions. Every person is obliged in conscience not to follow the directives of civil authorities when they are contrary to the demands of the moral order. Refusing obedience to civil authorities, when their demands are contrary to those of an upright conscience, finds its justification in the distinction between serving God and serving political authority. The criterion that stands out for guidance is to obey what is compatible to the fundamental values.

The obligation of the public sphere is to define the framework of the public conscience for all in order to avoid sectarianism. Such engagement is necessary and required because it obstructs approaches that intend to mandate a sectarian code. The role of religion in the public sphere is subject to socio-political critique that requires religious authorities to exercise caution in distinguishing principle from strategy. Experiences arising from various institutions have their place in the public sphere. Public sphere ought not to overlook any institution, because each institution brings richness to the common life. We have to rely on the process of rational exchange and search for a common ground. The meaning of truth will always be contested in the public sphere.

The relationship between religion and politics has caused endless dispute in the public sphere. The problem originates from the fact that which order should claim obedience and loyalty from believers. The situation has caused endless tension in the public sphere. The question of whether believers ought to grant allegiance to civil authority or religious authority is a crucial question, because a disordered person cannot make a balanced judgment.

Thomas Shannon, in search for a lasting solution, argues that a truthful obedience to conscience must be selective. For him, a selective obedience is founded upon one's conscience endowed with the ability to reject what is wrong and abide to what is right. Critics denounce selective obedience on the ground that it is sectarian, and as such it might cause political fragmentation and anarchy. From the perspective of human rights, however, selective obedience could be considered as a part of the freedom of conscience. It is the right of each person to challenge public policies that do not meet the demands of justice. Such a right is not a right to impose religious perspectives on others; rather, it is the right to advocate dialogue across institutions in search for a just public order.

There is no automatic obedience to any institution. The standard measure of conscience includes the ability to transcend institutional authority as well as the ability to discern in view of attaining the highest good. The role of religion includes the formation of conscience and corresponding moral responsibility of each person to act in conformity to one's own conscience.[22] Believers are expected to evaluate public policies from the perspective of religious conscience in view of building a better world. The concern for public morality to help people to form their conscience in accordance to what is right is paramount in public morality. The responsibility to make choices in public sphere rests with each individual, hoping that each person has a formed conscience.

The authority of conscience is closely related to public reason in the process of organizing political life. Public reason, as bearer of the truth and divine revelation, could be defined as a public sphere that provides a public framework able to facilitate arguments made in a transparent, free, and mutually justifiable way. Such understanding is founded upon the concepts of tolerance, mutual accommodation, public consensus, and the common good. Public reason is inclusive because it refers to the deepest level of moral values that determine the relationships between citizens. It deals with the challenge of how the political organization is to be understood. Public reason is public insofar as two variables, namely, freedom of choice and equality between citizens confirm that all citizens are subject to the public good and political justice. The two variables, according to John Rawls, help people to fulfill their civic duty toward each other.[23] People fulfill their duty of civility by supporting the idea of public reason. They become reasonable when viewing one another as free and equal in a system of mutual accommodation thereby offering "one another fair terms of cooperation according to what they consider the most reasonable conception of political justice."[24] That is to say the process of ordering a political community occurs when the two categories of human capability, public conscience and public reason, converge.

A standard public judgment is measured by public reason. Such a framework provides space for alternative thinking, creativity, and engagement between different categories of virtues. The public sphere becomes inclusive when it opens the door for people to appreciate the role of each institution, respect freedom of choice, and avoid hegemonic urge to dominate others. Public reason is authoritative in moral discourse because it is inclusive by the fact of appealing to the values that bind the political community together.[25] The accommodative character is an attribute that guarantees mutuality in social interaction. From the perspective of mutual accommodation, citizens' mutual knowledge of one another's identities expressed in the public sphere recognizes that the foundation of people's commitment to democratic ideals is anchored upon their loyalties toward public reason.[26] Inclusive public sphere entails accommodation of diversity. However, without common reference accepted at the beginning of political discourse, there cannot be a possibility of arriving at a reasonable form of consensus that could be considered necessary for the organization of the public life. In order to achieve civic friendship we need an inclusive public reason.

Public reason presupposes that individuals and groups are capable of pursuing a sense of the good as well as engage in reasonable discourse around the principles of justice and the common good. The concept of public reason, as a content of democracy, constitutes a sphere of communication through which the practice of justice becomes a public process open to all.[27] It is not a mere process of reasoning, but a regulative principle promoting standards that urge individuals to address public issues together. The dynamics of the public sphere cannot be limited to certain individuals, groups, and institutions; rather, it is the sum total of individuals, groups, and institutions. It locates the political process within various dimensions of political organization, culture, policymaking procedure, and the common good. A non-coercive process of opinion influences the political process from different perspectives.

The horizon of the public reason seeks to propagate a balanced understanding on socio-political interdependence by enhancing cooperation among people by accommodating diverse identities and inspire loyalty to the foundational ideals. The administrative structures must strive to reconcile differences, preserve order, and provide services to the people accordingly. This engagement, in search for political justice, requires a kind of impartiality among citizens and institutions.

Is it possible to construct a society of free and equal citizens divided by incompatible religious, philosophical, and ethical systems? This is a crucial question in the effort of organizing complex societies. A search for civic friendship goes beyond the destructive influence by advocating inclusive democracy and engaged pluralism open to all perspectives without restriction. The principle of overlapping consensus, claims John Rawls, assumes that individuals and groups are capable of pursuing a sense of the common good in an engaged reasonable discourse and cooperation around the principle of justice.[28] The convergence of public conscience and public reason in the public sphere confirms that the process of political integration requires the practice of justice.

Religious Virtues and Civic Virtues

The formation of public conscience presupposes an integration of religious virtues and civic virtues. Mature religious people living in circumstances fashioned by free interaction and pluralism seek a balance between the attitudes grounded in religion and values grounded in general sphere of humanity. In pluralist societies, people are expected to be sensitive not only to the overlapping moral views but also to moral disagreements. In many ways, one's view is supported by secular grounds that people of any religious persuasion can accept, even if appealing to those grounds entail revising one's own traditions.[29]

Religious virtues and civic virtues are intrinsically interconnected. Such a natural occurrence supports the claim that religious virtues could be interpreted as a content of civic virtues. In a pluralist society, civic virtue refers to the dynamics of taking reasonable position on important issues related to the process of resolving problems with others that count as a responsible political participation. I have already suggested that there is an overlap between the content of religiously-based obligations and secularly-based moral obligations. There is a substantial overlap between the basic moral principles such as those that prohibit murder, theft, and dishonesty. The integration of religious virtues and civic virtues is evident in Mother Theresa's works of compassion, because her practice of the religious virtue of compassion manifests civic virtue. Such observation confirms that Mother Teresa exercised both religious virtues and civic virtues in her works of compassion. We can also argue that the religious requirement to love one's neighbor as oneself brings together two categories of virtues: religious virtues and civic virtues.

It is possible to arrive at normative claims that overcome the divisiveness by establishing institutions of moral formation.[30] Arguments that are general enough to count as good reasons are good to be entrained within the public sphere. The challenge, however, lies with the assumption that arguments from religion must undergo refinement in order to attain legitimacy within the public sphere.[31] Religious contribution may have some impact in the public sphere insofar as they are translated into general public language. The point under consideration here is that religious import must be subjected to the dynamics of secularism to enhance a balanced interaction. The challenge brought forward here refers to the ability of making a religious contribution understood by all, believers and non-believers alike. That is to say every citizen must acknowledge that inclusive language goes beyond the institutional threshold that divides the public sphere.[32] This argument does not intend to enforce secularism, but enhance the need of using a language that is inclusive.

Without that the religious import could be interpreted as self-centered and sectarian.

A political misunderstanding is caused by the lack of reasonable conversation. Such a situation occurs when people cease to engage each other in a reasonable way. An argument ceases to be civil when it becomes dominated by prejudice; when its vocabulary becomes premised on the assumption that my insight is unique; when the parties to the conversation cease to listen to one another, or hear only what they want to hear, or see other's argument through the screen of their own categories. When things like this happen, then, people cannot engage one another in a rational argument. Conversation becomes quarrelsome when there is no rational exchange of ideas.[33] Public discourse furnishes the required standards by furnishing a common universe of discourse in which public issues are intelligibly argued, thereby building a consensus, which is the objective of the public discourse.

The formation of public conscience and transformation of public institutions require transformation of the minds and hearts of individuals and communities. In such a process the whole transformation of social relationships is accomplished in an orderly fashion through the concerted effort of individuals and groups guided by their conscience. Transformation of the individual must precede social transformation. Such a perspective will eventually promote behavioral change and transformative actions. Transformation at this level is more effective than political campaigns, pressured reforms, revolutions, and multiplication of laws because it deals with the reform of the person from inside. As such, a believer ought to promise relative loyalty to the state as well as be prepared to condemn civil injustice. It is therefore justified for a believer to reject absolute loyalty to any institution, ideology, or tradition.

Virtues are cultivated by listening to what the other person has to say as well as use one's imagination to uncover new ways of mutual understanding. We are urged to recognize the otherness of the other by resisting the temptation to reduce others to our own categories. We must strive to enlarge our horizon, engage in self-criticism, and be willing to transform our views in light of shared encounter. A healthy public sphere is one that brings together diverse perspectives emerging from different institutions. It is destructive to advocate exclusion of any institution from the public sphere; instead, we must promote inclusive democracy that accommodates diverse institutions and perspectives. In search for a balanced approach that can enhance mutual enrichment between institutions, we have to make sure that there is dialogue and integration between religious virtues and civic virtues.

A convergence of various categories of virtues is a political process since it provides space for sharing various conceptions of the good in the process of decision-making. The challenge to social transformation is encountered by the challenge to cast out clear, imagination, virtue, and commitment for the future. The challenge of imagination is important because national projects, politics, and economic planning lack creativity. Irresponsible governance is caused by the lack of political imagination. The question we have to ask ourselves is: which forms of imagination and creativity should be introduced in order to enhance socio-political transformation? The following discussion provides insights that illuminate the process of responding to the question.

Imagination and Creativity

There is discussion in almost every dimension of human experience and institution about paradigm shift in directing humanity toward a new future. This kind of desire attempts to take seriously the capacity of human being to solicit possibilities that have not yet been actualized. Creative imagination enhances awareness of what the future could be on condition of human creativity. The idea of paradigm shift refers to the virtue of hope and search for change. Reason-guided search solicit creative imagination to invent paradigms that can address prevailing challenges of life. It is a shift from the status quo that embarks on the search for new possibilities in terms of ethical reflection geared to promote change. The impulse of the spirit working instinctively in the conscience of the informed persons will always extend beyond the readymade traditions by suggesting unexplored avenues of ethical imagination. Ability to formulate paradigms that can shape the future depends on creative thinking sustained by imagination and desire to transform social conditions of life.

Imagination is a creative process that goes to the depth of reality. It is a powerful variable that penetrates the reality with an expectation of discovering creative paradigms. It is, however, essential to note that imagination is not the same as fantasy. Fantasy is a flight from historical reality to a world where we create non-historical realities. For the sake of grasping the reality, imagination, creativity, and virtue direct us toward the depth of thought and creativity that involve a profound engagement with historical reality. It is an analysis that goes beneath the surface. The starting point for political imagination must be what is real, that is, what is concretely thought to be experienced in a given context of life.

Creativity is the most required initiative in the present time, because it is identified with the process of finding alternatives to the prevailing challenges that seem to propagate hopelessness. What we need is to open the whole range of human mind. Sometimes we do not know what to choose, and whatever we choose is ineffective; and the choices we make appear to be fruitless because we do not want to think creatively. Most often there is a way out, but such a possibility requires an effort of imagination that involves an ability to envision alternative models of thinking and acting.

Restructuring of traditions comes from a creative mind and transformative imaginations. Creative thinking is basically related to the power of imagination endowed with the ability to cultivate the power of human spirit, rationality, and consciousness. Without imagination there cannot be dream for the future. For this reason, the ability to create imaginations is a source of creative power.[34] Imagination is attached to the power of mind, inspiration of the spirit, and desire to change for the better. Creativity is not limited to the experience emerging from a single institution; rather, it has to emerge from all dimensions of human experience.

The ethics of participatory governance and democratic accountability are founded upon the power of imagination and creativity. These foundations are sometimes neglected within the political discourse when the dynamics of governance remain stuck at the level of patronage and authoritarianism. The art of social organization is far from meeting the challenge of pluralism. If democracy is perceived as an attitude of mind, then it is fitting to pay due attention to the formation of citizens. Such engagement entails recapturing the spirit of learning and critical thinking for the sake of self-transformation. Creative thinking challenges status quo and uniformity. Socio-political change cannot be a once-and-for-all phenomenon; rather, it has to be an ongoing process of self-transformation founded upon principles of participation, critical thinking, and creative imagination.

Political imagination is not just to conform to the prevailing traditions; rather, it is a process of evaluating the prevailing conditions of life in a wider context in search of alternative paradigms. It is a process that is more than presenting a chronology of socio-political events. Imagination is a means through which political thinkers attempt to express fundamental values that transcend immediate needs and private interests. A number of political thinkers acknowledge that they inject imagination into their theories. They do so because they believe that their ideas enable them to see things that are not apparent to others. For them, imagination is significant because political philosophy must be committed toward lessening the gap between the possibilities grasped through political imagination and actualities of political existence.[35] Creative imagination, as an aspect of political thinking, provides a way to think about political society from the perspective of civic virtues, which is a necessary complement to social action. It is an attempt to take political challenges seriously by trying to understand the nature of a human person vis-à-vis changing conditions of life.

The need of creative imagination within socio-political dynamics requires us to think creatively in search for effective paradigms of social organization. Imagination enables us to place one's dreams beyond the scope of political events. It is a process that refers to the human potential expressed in terms of intuition. The central question explored by visionary people is whether substantive change in a democratic polity is possible and whether some alternative answers could be found. A profound vision acknowledges pluralistic politics that combines features of religious virtues with civic virtues, private and public interests, and diversity of experience and interests in favor of promoting participation and inclusion. It is a process that advocates innovative perspectives and preferences that will eventually seep into the balancing process affecting the shape of political organization.[36] Political imagination unveils localized cultural narrative as well as transformative ideas. Such a process requires creative minds accompanied by transformative imaginations.

The strongest political organization takes on an imaginative dimension that enables the individual to relate emotionally and cognitively to the others. With such a background, imagination becomes a creative power of intellect as a whole. Imaginative initiatives attempt to surpass the immediacy by soliciting hope and transformation. Creative imagination magnifies the experience of reality by playing the role of discovery. There is a danger of thinking that the imaginative basis of belief can be detached from historical experience.[37] Ways of believing and thinking that detach themselves from concrete experience become sterile and irrelevant.

The dynamics of imagination and creativity helps us to penetrate the reality. It is a process that requires attention by extending human experience to the level of discovery. The moral significance of human life is not limited to the tendency of moving from one social problem to another; rather, it moves towards ultimate questions of existence and truth. The situation derives from the fact that human actions are fields of self-determination, meaning that goodness of persons is not automatic but a quality acquired through self-cultivation. The horizon of imagination requires us to challenge ourselves as well as penetrate the reality of experience, including the socio-political experience. The horizon of these variables defines the sphere of political imagination. Imagination and creativity are essential attributes in the process of identifying alternative paradigms of social transformation.

Significant political forms are founded upon moral experience of the community, which derive from the exercise of civic virtues. The dynamics of a virtue require people to dream, create, and effect change to improve life conditions. Imagination is the source of insights required for creativity, because it motivates the spirit of commitment and transformation. Such awareness focuses on forming people of service for the community, which entails self-sacrifice for others.

Conclusion

The discussion began by presenting public values as guidance for public morality and political integration. Such a perspective aimed at discouraging ethnocentric attitude and imposition of private convictions on others. The discussion went on to argue that political integration cannot become reality without infusing rational dialogue in the public sphere as well as focus on the formation of citizens by cultivating various categories of virtues. To this end, the idea of overlapping consensus becomes constructive on condition that it accommodates diversity of identities, loyalties, and interests. The overlapping consensus must be considered as a common denominator built upon the effort of bringing together diverse experiences of participation and interest. Such engagement went as far as proposing imagination and creativity as a means of bringing about social transformation. Such an argument was deliberately brought forward to challenge modalities of leadership and governance founded upon blood relationships.

Notes

[1] On the meaning of human dignity I am indebted to the insights of Alan D. Falconer, "Human Dignity," *Dictionary of Christian Ethics* (Philadelphia: Westminster Press, 1986), 278-279.

[2] Such a claim confirms that human rights, with ontological essence, are also conferred to the process of historicization, meaning that human rights are grounded in human nature and social practice. A detailed elaboration to this insight is found in the work of Nicholas Wolterstorff, *Justice: Rights and Wrongs* (Princeton, New Jersey: Princeton University Press, 2008), 313-324.

[3] Jack Donnelly, "The Relative Universality of Human Rights," *Human Rights Quarterly,* 29, 2 (May, 2007): 281-306, at 288.

[4] Ignacio Ellacuria, "Human Rights in a Divided Society," in Alfred Hennelly, S.J., and John Langan, S.J., eds., *Human Rights in the Americas: The Struggle for Consensus* (Washington, D.C.: Georgetown University Press, 1982), 52-65, at 59.

[5] Pope John Paul II, "Respect for Human Rights: The Secret of True Peace," *http://www.nccbuscc.org/sdwp/international/humanrights* (Accessed on March 30, 2010).

[6] Francis Fukuyama, *The End of History and the Last Man* (New York: Avon Books, Inc., 1992), 322 – 327.

[7] David P. Forsythe, *Human Rights in International Relations* (Cambridge: Cambridge University Press, 2000), 28-52. See also R. J. Vincent, *Human Rights and International Relations* (Cambridge: Cambridge University Press, 1986), 35; David Jacobson, *Rights Across Borders: Immigration and the Decline of Citizenship* (Baltimore: John Hopkins University Press, 1995), 72.

[8] Pope Paul VI, *Mater et Magistra* (Nairobi: St. Paul Publications, 1990), 65.

[9] Stanley Hauerwas, *Vision and Virtue* (Notre Dame, Indiana: University of Notre Dame Press, 1974), 237.

[10] Ibid., 236.

[11] Ibid., 238.

[12] David Hollenbach, S.J., *The Common Good and Christian Ethics* (Cambridge, Massachusetts: Cambridge University Press, 2002), 3.

[13] James Donahue and Theresa M. Moser, eds., *Religion, Ethics, and the Common Good* (Connecticut: Twenty-Third Publications, 1996), vii-ix, at x.

[14] William R. O'Neill, "Reason and the Common Good," in Donahue and Moser, eds., *Religion, Ethics, and the Common Good*, 71-72.

[15] Ellacuria, "Human Rights in a Divided Society," 64.

[16] Human rights are a form of moral entitlement that applies to all people at all times and in all situations and cultures. For further elaboration, see L.W. Sumner, *The Moral Foundation of Rights* (Oxford: Oxford University Press, 1987), 13.

[17] Jeffrey Stout, "The Spirit of Democracy and the Rhetoric of Excess," *Journal of Religious Ethics*, 35, 1 (March, 2007): 3-20, at 5.

[18] Abbot W. M., ed., *The Documents of the Second Vatican Council* (New York: Guild Press, 1966), Gaudium et Spes, 16.

[19] Pope John Paul II, "Address of World Day of Peace," Cited in Frank Brennan, *Acting on Conscience: How Can We Responsibly Mix Religion and Politics?* (Queensland: Queensland University Press, 2007), 38.

[20] Abbot, *The Documents of the Second Vatican Council*, Gaudium et Spes, 16.

[21] Thomas Shannon, *Render Unto God: A Theology of Selective Obedience* (New York: Paulist Press, 1974).

[22] United States Council of Catholic Bishops, "Forming Consciences for Faithful Citizenship," *Origins*, 37, 25 (November, 2007): 5.

[23] John Rawls, *The Law of Peoples* (Cambridge, Massachusetts: Harvard University Press, 2001), 132.

[24] Ibid., 136.

[25] Charles Larmore, "Public Reason," in Samuel Freeman ed., *The Cambridge Companion to Rawls* (Cambridge: Cambridge University Press, 2002), 574.

[26] Ibid., 153.

[27] An approach that present democracy as an exercise of public reason is found in the work of Amartya Sen, *The Idea of Justice* (Cambridge, Massachusetts: Belknap Press, 2009), 324. See also the works of Jürgen Habermas, *The Structural Transformation of the Public Sphere* (Cambridge, Massachusetts: MIT Press, 1989); Joshua Cohen and Joel Rogers, eds., *On Democracy* (London: Penguin, 1983); Ronald Dworkin, *Is Democracy Possible Here? Principles for a New Political Debate* (Princeton, New Jersey: Princeton University Press, 2006).

[28] John Rawls, *A Theory of Justice* (Boston: Oxford University Press, 1971), 78.

[29] Robert Audi and Nicholas Wolterstorff, *Religion in the Public Square: The Place of Religious Convictions in Political Debate* (Lanham, Maryland: Rawman and Littlefield, 1997), 14-15.

[30] Phil Enns, "Habermas, Reason, and the Problem of Religion: The Role of Religion in the Public Sphere," *http://www.blackwell-synergy.com/doi/full/10.1111/j.1468-2265.2007.00347.x?presearah=* (Accessed on March 14, 2010).

[31] Ibid., 12.

[32] Ibid., 13.

[33] John Courtney Murray, *We Hold These Truths: Catholic Reflections on the American Proposition* (New York: Sheed and Ward, 1960), 14

[34] Bernard Cooke, *Power and the Spirit of God: Toward an Experience-Based Pneumatology* (New York: Oxford University Press, 2004), 104.

[35] Hauerwas, *Vision and Virtue*, 224-225.

[36] Ibid., 230.

[37] Aylward Shorter, *Christianity and the African Imagination: African Synod Resources for Inculturation* (Nairobi: St. Paul Publications, 1996), 17.

Bibliography

Abbot, W. M. ed. *The Documents of the Second Vatican Council.* New York: Guild Press, 1966.

Ake, Claude. *Democracy and Development in Africa.* Washington, D.C.: The Brookings Institution, 1996.

Amaladoss, Michael. "Religions for Peace." *America* (December, 2001): 6-8.

AMECEA Plenary Conference. "Building Christian Communities in Eastern Africa." *AFER*, 18, 5 (October, 1976).

AMECEA Study Conference. "Planning for the Church in Eastern Africa in 1980s." *AFER* 16, 1 (February, 1974): 1-32.

Appleby, Scott, R. *The Ambivalence of the Sacred: Religion, Violence, and Reconciliation.* New York: Rawman and Littlefield, 2000.

Audi, Robert and Wolterstorff, Nicholas. *Religion in the Public Square: The Place of Religious Convictions in Political Debate.* New York: Rowman and Littlefield Publishers, 1997.

Avineri, Shlomo and de-Shalit, Aviner eds. *Communitarianism and Individualism.* Oxford: Oxford University Press, 1992.

Banks, A. James. "Diversity, Group Identity, and Citizenship Education in a Global Age." *Educational Researcher*, 37, 3 (April, 2008): 129-139.

Bayart, Jean-François. *The State in Africa: The Politics of the Belly.* London: Longman, 1993.

Bednar, Jenna ed. *A Political Theory of Federalism.* London: Stanford Institute of International Studies, 1999.

Bellah, Robert et al. *Habits of the Heart: Individualism and Commitment in American Life.* San Francisco: Harper & Row, 1985.

Benhabib, Seyla ed. *Democracy and Difference.* New Jersey: Princeton University Press, 1996.

Berman, Bruce et al., eds. *Ethnicity and Democracy in Africa.* London: James Currey Ltd, 2004.

Bloemraad, Irene et al. "Citizenship and Immigration: Multiculturalism, Assimilation, and Challenges to the

Nation-State." *Annual Review of Sociology*, 34 (August, 2008): 153-179.

Brennan, Frank *Acting on Conscience*: *How Can We Responsibly Mix Religion and Politics?* Queensland: Queensland University Press, 2007.

Browen Manby, *Struggles for Citizenship in Africa*. London: Zed Books Limited, 2009.

Catholic Bishops of Kenya. *On the Road to Democracy*. Nairobi: St. Paul Publications, 1994.

_____. *Our Social Responsibility*. Nairobi: St. Paul Publications, 1996.

Christians, G. Clifford et al. *Normative Theories of the Media*: *Journalism in Democratic Societies*. Chicago: University of Illinois Press, 2009.

Coakley, John ed. *The Territorial Management of Ethnic Conflict*. London: Frank Cass, 1993.

Cochrane, James et al., eds. *Facing the Truth*: *South African Faith Communities and the Truth and Reconciliation Commission*. Cape Town: David Philip Publishers Limited, 1999.

Cohen, Abner. *The Politics of Elite Culture*: *Explorations in the Dramaturgy of Power in a Modern African Society*. Berkeley, California: University of California Press, 1981.

Cohen, Joshua and Rogers, Joel eds. *On Democracy*. London: Penguin, 1983.

Cooke, Bernard. *Power and the Spirit of God*: *Toward an Experience-Based Pneumatology*. New York: Oxford University Press, 2004.

Crawford, Young ed. *Ethnic Diversity and Public Policy*: *An Overview*. Geneva: Macmillan, 1998.

Crocker, A. Chester et al., eds. *Turbulent Peace*: *The Challenges of Managing International Conflict*. Washington, D.C.: United States Institute of Peace Press, 2001.

Dahl, A. Robert. *Pluralist Democracy in the United States*: *Conflict and Consent*. Chicago: Rand McNally, 1967.

De Gruchy, W. John and Martin, William Stephen, eds. *Religion and the Reconstruction of Civil Society*. Pretoria: University of South Africa, 1995.

Donahue, James and Moser, M. Theresa eds. *Religion, Ethics, and the Common Good.* Connecticut: Twenty-Third Publications, 1996.

Donnelly, Jack. "The Relative Universality of Human Rights." *Human Rights Quarterly,* 29, 2 (May, 2007): 281-306.

Dulles, Avery. "Christ among the Religions." *America* (May, 2000): 14-22.

Dworkin, Ronald. *Is Democracy Possible Here? Principles for a New Political Debate.* Princeton, New Jersey: Princeton University Press, 2006.

Ellis, Stephen ed. *Africa Now: People, Policies, and Institutions.* London: James Currey and Heinemann, 1996.

Enlund, Harri and Nyamnjoh, B. Francis eds. *Rights and the Politics of Recognition in Africa.* London: Zed Books, 2004.

Forsythe, P. David. *Human Rights in International Relations.* Cambridge: Cambridge University Press, 2000.

Fukuyama, Francis. *The End of History and the Last Man.* New York: Avon Books, Inc., 1992.

Glickman, Harvey ed. *Ethnic Conflict and Democratization in Africa.* Atlanta: The African Studies Association Press, 1995.

Gregory, L. Jones et al., eds. *God, Truth, and Witness: Engaging Stanley Hauerwas.* Michigan: Grand Rapids, 2005.

Gustavsson, Sverker and Lewin, Leif eds. *The Future of the Nation-State: Essays on Cultural Pluralism and Political Integration.* New York: Routledge, 1996.

Gurr, T. Ted. "People against States: Ethno-Political Conflict and the Changing World System." *International Studies Quarterly,* 38 (September, 1994): 347-377.

Gyekye, Kwame. *Tradition and Modernity: Philosophical Reflections on the African Experience.* New York: Oxford University Press, 1997.

Habermas, Jürgen *Moral Consciousness and Communicative Action.* Cambridge, Massachusetts: The MIT Press, 1991.

_____. *The Structural Transformation of the Public Sphere.* Cambridge, Massachusetts: MIT Press, 1989.

Halstead, Mark J. ed. *Education in Morality*. London: Routledge, 1999.

Harbeson, W. John, et al. eds. *Civil Society and State in Africa*. Boulder, Colorado: Lynne Rienner Publishers, 1994.

Hastings, Adrian. *The Construction of Nationhood: Ethnicity, Religion, and Nationalism*. Cambridge: Cambridge University Press, 1997.

Hauerwas, Stanley. *Vision and Virtue*. Notre Dame, Indiana: Notre Dame University Press, 1974.

Haughey, C. John ed. *Personal Values in Public Policy*. New York: Paulist Press, 1979.

Helmick, G. Raymond and Petersen, L. Rodney eds. *Forgiveness and Reconciliation: Religion, Public Policy, and Conflict Transformation*. Philadelphia: Templeton Press, 2001.

Hennelly, Alfred and Langan, John eds. *Human Rights in the Americas: The Struggle for Consensus*. Washington, D.C.: Georgetown University Press, 1982.

Herman, Bakris. *Federalism and the Role of the State*. Toronto: Toronto University Press, 1987.

Hollenbach, David ed. *Driven from Home: Protecting the Rights of Forced Migrants*. Washington, D.C.: Georgetown University Press, 2010.

_____. "Religion and Political Life." *Theological Studies*, 52, 1 (March, 1991): 87-106.

_____. "Report from Rwanda: An Interview with Augustine Karekezi." *America* (December 7, 1996): 13-17.

_____. *The Common Good and Christian Ethics*. Cambridge, Massachusetts: Cambridge University Press, 2002.

_____. *The Global Face of Public Faith: Politics, Human Rights, and Christian Ethics*. Washington, D.C.: Georgetown University Press, 2003.

Hutchinson, John and Smith, D. Anthony eds. *Ethnicity*. New York: Oxford University Press, 1996.

Idowu, William. "Ethnicity, Ethnicism, and Citizenship: A Philosophical Reflection on the African Experience." *Journal of Social Sciences*, 8, 1 (January, 2004): 45-58.

Ihonvbere, O. Julius. *Economic Crisis, Civil Society, and Democratization*: The Case of Zambia. Asmara: Africa World Press, 1996.

Jacobson, David. *Rights Across Borders*: Immigration and the Decline of Citizenship (Baltimore: John Hopkins University Press, 1995).

Josiah, Royce. *The Philosophy of Loyalty*. New York: The McMillan Company, 1924.

Juergensmeyer, Mark. *Terror in the Mind of God*: The Global Rise of Religious Violence. Berkeley, California: University of California Press, 2000.

K'Ahenda, Sewe ed. *A Theological Response to the Tragedy of Refugees and Internally Displaced Persons in Africa*. Nairobi: CUEA Publications, 2007.

Kimenyi, S. Mwangi. *Ethnic Diversity, Liberty, and the State*: The African Dilemma. Boston: Edward Elgar, 1997.

Koigi wa Wamwere. *Negative Ethnicity*: From Bias to Genocide. New York: Seven Stories Press, 2003.

Konate, A. Siendou. "The Politics of Identity and Violence in Côte d'Ivoire." *West Africa Review*, 5 (February, 2004): 1-15.

Kouassi, N'Guettia. "The Itinerary of the African Integration." *African Integration Review*, 1, 2 (July, 2007): 1-22.

Lamb, David. *The Africans* (New York: Vintage Books, 1984).

Loyd, C. Brown-John ed. *Centralizing and Decentralizing Trends in Federal States*. Lanham, Maryland: University Press of America, 1988.

MacIntyre, Alasdair. *Dependent Rational Animals*: Why Human Beings Need the Virtues. Illinois: Carus Publishing Company, 1999.

Magesa, Laurenti. *African Religion in the Dialogue Debate*: From Intolerance to Coexistence. Zweigniederlssung, Zurich: Lit Verlag, 2010.

Mamdani, Mahmood. *Citizen and Subject*: Contemporary Africa and the Legacy of Late Colonialism. New Jersey: Princeton University Press, 1996.

_____. *When Victims Become Killers*: Colonialism, Nativity, and the Genocide. New Jersey: Princeton University Press, 2001.

Markham, S. Ian. *Plurality and Christian Ethics*. Cambridge, Massachusetts: Cambridge University Press, 1994.

Mbiti, John. *African Religions and Philosophy*. Oxford: Heinemann Educational Publishers, 1969.

Mejia, Rodrigo ed. *The Conscience of Society*. Nairobi: St. Paul Publications, 1995.

Mugambi, Jesse N. K. and Nasimiyu-Wasike, Anne eds. *Moral and Ethical Issues in African Christianity*. Nairobi: Initiative Publishers, 1992.

Murray, Courtney John. *We Hold These Truths*: *Catholic Reflections on the American Proposition*. New York: Sheed and Ward, 1960.

Ndegwa, N. Stephen. "Citizenship and Ethnicity: An Examination of Two Transition Moments in Kenyan Politics." *American Political Science Review*, 91, 3 (June, 1997): 599-615.

Neuhaus, John Richard. *The Naked Public Square*: *Religion and Democracy*. Michigan: William B. Eerdmans Publishing Company, 1984.

Niebuhr, Reinhold. *The Children of the Light and the Children of the Darkness*. New York: Charles Scribner's Sons, 1944.

Nyamnjoh, B. Francis. "From Bounded to Flexible Citizenship: Lessons from Africa." *Citizenship Studies*, 11, 1 (February, 2007): 73-82.

O'Connor, Anthony *The African City*. London: Hutchinson University Library for Africa, 1983.

Oginga Odinga, Jaramogi. *Not Yet Uhuru*: *An Autobiography of Oginga Odinga*. London: Heinemann Educational Books, 1967.

Okullu, Henry. *Church and Politics in East Africa*. Nairobi: Uzima Press Limited, 1987.

Otieno, Nicholas. *Human Rights and Social Justice in Africa*. Nairobi: All Africa Conference of Churches, 2007.

Page, Ruth. *Ambiguity and the Presence of God*. London: SCM, 1985.

Pope, Paul VI. *Mater et Magistra* (Nairobi: St. Paul Publications, 1990).

Rawls, John. *A Theory of Justice*. Boston: Oxford University Press, 1971.

_____. *The Law of Peoples.* Cambridge, Massachusetts: Harvard University Press, 2001.

Rosenfield, Raymond ed. *The Challenges of Federalism: USA, USSR, and Ukraine.* Kyiv: National Academy of Public Administration Office of the President of Ukraine, 2008.

Rothchild, Donald and Olorunsola, V. A., eds. *State Versus Ethnic Claims: African Policy Dilemmas.* Boulder, Colorado: Westview Press, 1983.

_____. *Managing Ethnic Conflict in Africa.* Washington, D.C.: Brookings Institution Press, 1997.

Rufus, S. Davis. *The Federal Principle.* Berkeley, California: University of California Press, 1978.

Sandel, J. Michael. *Justice: What's the Right Thing to Do?* New York: Farrar, Straus, and Giroux, 2009.

Sanks, T. Howland. *Salt, Leaven, and Light: The Community Called Church.* New York: Crossroad, 1992.

Sen, Amartya. *The Idea of Justice.* Cambridge, Massachusetts: Belknap Press, 2009.

Shannon, Thomas. *Render Unto God: A Theology of Selective Obedience.* New York: Paulist Press, 1974.

Sharkey, J. Heather. "Arab Identity and Ideology in Sudan: The Politics of Language, Ethnicity, and Race." *African Affairs,* 107, 426 (December, 2007): 21-43.

Shorter, Aylward. *Christianity and the African Imagination: African Synod Resources for Inculturation.* Nairobi: St. Paul Publications, 1996.

Shue, Henry. Subsistence, *Affluence, and US Foreign Policy.* (New Jersey: Princeton University Press, 1980.

Stephen N. Ndegwa, "Citizenship and Ethnicity: An Examination of Two Transition Moments in Kenyan Politics." *The American Political Science Review,* 91, 3 (September, 1997): 599-616.

Stout, Jeffrey. "The Spirit of Democracy and the Rhetoric of Excess." *Journal of Religious Ethics,* 35, 1 (March, 2007): 3-20.

Swanson, Tod. "The Persuasive Voice of Oscar Romero." *Journal of Religious Ethics,* 29, 3 (Spring, 2001): 127-144.

Tangaza Occasional Papers, *Ethnicity: Blessing or Curse*. Nairobi: St. Paul Publications, 1999.

Tarimo, Aquiline. "The Extended Family and the Cycle of Poverty." *African Christian Studies*, 20, 2 (June, 2004): 5-32.

Tordoff, William. *Government and Politics in Africa*. Indianapolis: Indiana University Press, 1984.

Tordoff, William. *Government and Politics in Africa*. Indianapolis: Indiana University Press, 1993.

United States Council of Catholic Bishops, "Forming Consciences for Faithful Citizenship." *Origins*, 37, 25 (November, 2007): 5 – 6.

Ury, William. *Getting to Peace*. New York: The Penguin Group, 1999.

Veney, R. Cassandra. *Forced Migration in Eastern Africa: Democratization, Structural Adjustment, and Refugees*. Pennsylvania: Palgrave MacMillan, 2006.

Vincent, R. J. *Human Rights and International Relations*. Cambridge: Cambridge University Press, 1986.

Walzer, Michael. *Spheres of Justice: A Defense of Pluralism and Equality*. New York: Basic Books, 1993.

Warioba, Joseph. "The Report of the Warioba Commission on Corruption." *Business Times, Tanzania* (June 27, 1997): i-xxxiii.

Wrong, Michela. *It's Our Turn to Eat: The Story of a Kenyan Whistle-Blower*. New York: HarperCollins Publishers, 2009.

Wuthnow, Robert. *Christianity and Civil Society: The Contemporary Debate*. Valley Forge, Pennsylvania: Trinity Press International, 1996.

Young, Marion Iris. *Justice and the Politics of Difference*. New Jersey: Princeton University Press, 1990.

_____. *Inclusion and Democracy*. Oxford: Oxford University Press, 2000.